The Search for Meaning

THE SEARCH FOR MEANING

Myth and Mystery
in the New Millennium

by
Robert J. Hater

A Crossroad Book
The Crossroad Publishing Company
New York

The Author and Publisher wish to acknowledge their gratitude for permission to quote material from the following:

Leonard J. Biallas, *Myths, gods, heroes, and saviors.* Copyright © 1986 by Leonard J. Biallas. Published by Twenty-Third Publications, Mystic, Conn. 06355. Reprinted with permission of the publisher.

Tom F. Driver, *The Magic of Ritual.* Copyright © 1991. Reprinted with the permission of HarperCollins Publishers.

Richard L. Sartore, ed. *Joseph Campbell on Myth and Mythology.* Copyright © 1994. Reprinted with the permission of University Press of America.

The Individual and His Religion, by Gordon W. Allport. Copyright © 1950 by Macmillan Publishing Company; copyright renewed © 1978 by Robert B. Allport. Reprinted with the permission of Simon & Schuster.

Identity and the Sacred: A Sketch for a New Social-Scientific Theory of Religion, by Hans Mol. Copyright © 1976 by Hans Mol. First American Edition published by The Free Press, a Division of Simon & Schuster. Reprinted with permission of the publisher.

Roger Schmidt, *Exploring Religion,* 2nd ed., © 1980, 1988 by Wadsworth Publishing Company. Used by permission of the publisher.

1998
The Crossroad Publishing Company
370 Lexington Avenue, New York, NY 10017

Printed in the United States of America

Library of Congress Cataloging-in-Publication Data

Hater, Robert J.
    The search for meaning : myth and mystery in the new millennium /
    Robert J. Hater.
            p.   cm.
    Includes bibliographical references.
    ISBN 0-8245-1692-3 (pbk.)
    1. Religion.   2. Hater, Robert J.   3. Religion—Forecasting.
I. Title.
BL48.H362   1998
200—dc21   97-27323
                                            CIP

Dedications

To my loving parents, Stanley and Olivia Hater
The stories told in this book are a tribute to your love.

Dad, you died in 1980,
but your presence, commitment, and love
remain with me.

Mom, at eighty-six years of age,
you continue to inspire me
through your love, intelligence,
support, and wisdom.
Thanks for reading this manuscript
and offering me valuable suggestions.
You are great!

To Geraldine Cain,
Marie Antoine Humpert, S.C.,
Jeanette Jabour, O.P.,
and Diana Stano, O.S.U.
Your encouragement, advice, and friendship
while I wrote this book are very much appreciated.
Thank you very much.

Contents

Acknowledgments

I am grateful to the University of Dayton for the sabbatical that enabled me to write this book. Special thanks are given to Dr. William P. Roberts and Dr. William P. Anderson, colleagues in the Religious Studies Department, who read the manuscript and offered many valuable comments.

I express deep appreciation to Eva Solomon, C.S.J., for her wisdom, friendship, and advice regarding the Ojibway people, their stories and traditions.

In particular, I thank Dr. C. Walker Gollar, Assistant Professor of Theology at Xavier University, Cincinnati, Ohio, for his very careful analysis of this book's content and style. His suggestions helped me greatly as I prepared the final draft.

Introduction

I recently transferred my property and savings to a trust account. This involved lawyers, financial advisors, tax consultants, phone calls, deeds, stocks, and savings accounts. After four months, the process was almost completed. For some unknown reason, I never closed out two small savings accounts. One afternoon, I decided to do so. I drove to the Cheviot Building and Loan Company. As I approached it, emotion welled up within me. The feelings became more pronounced, as I entered the building. Suddenly, my thoughts flashed back forty-three years to my junior year in high school. I saw myself entering the same building to deposit money in the first account I opened by myself.

Over the years, the money fluctuated. At this time, I had five hundred dollars left. Nervously, I told the teller to close the account. In a few moments, it was done. I walked out with a check to put into my trust. I felt lousy. One smaller account of $137.38 remained. My nervousness intensified as I drove five miles to the Centennial Savings Bank, formerly the Glenway Loan and Deposit Company. A block from my destination, I stopped for a traffic light and glanced at the savings book. Its old cover depicted a picture of the Glenway Loan and Deposit Company in its original location. Seeing it, I was filled with a powerful emotional surge. I sat at the light more puzzled and insecure than ever.

Not aware of what was happening, I pulled from the road and turned off the car. As I looked again at the old book, I suddenly remembered my early childhood and uncovered a memory that long since had disappeared from consciousness.

I was four or five years old. I felt my father's hand holding mine, as we walked down Glenway Avenue to the building that was pictured on the old book. We went in. I watched Dad sign papers and followed him to the bank teller. Dad said we were opening my account and encouraged me to save pennies and nickels to put into it. Dad and I went into this same building many other times to deposit money.

I looked at the old book and thought, "I can't close this account! It means too much to me." The $137.38 was all that remained from many transactions completed during the past fifty-six years, beginning when Dad and I walked hand in hand down Glenway Avenue to open it. I now understood my strong emotions about this book and the account I had just closed. They were more than old savings books; they symbolized something too deep to convey adequately.

Starting my car, I drove to the Centennial Savings Bank. I told the teller to keep this account intact, use the old book, and transfer it into my trust. I only wanted the name on the book changed from Robert J. Hater to Robert J. Hater Trust. Puzzled, she looked at me, realizing the inconvenience of transferring this small amount into a trust.

I thought, "I am not going to explain to her what is happening inside me." After I repeated my request, she obliged. I walked out of the building and loan, relieved and happy, holding my old book. From a logical point of view, what I did made little sense, but from a mythical perspective it made all the sense in the world.

The new millennium will require fresh ways of thinking and acting. It challenges us to respond with a better appreciation of the deep currents that motivate us. With such knowledge we can move beyond this earthly "Eden" to acknowledge our place in the universe.

My experience with the savings book goes to the heart of what it means to be human. It seems as if my father's spirit guided me through this profound experience to teach me that life's deepest level goes beyond figures, money, and facts to the mythical reality of what it means to be alive.

The Search for Meaning invites us to examine the meaning of our lives. This book reflects on our stories and experiences in light of our myths, symbols, and rituals. Thirty years ago, while teaching a course at the College of Mount Saint Joseph in Cincinnati, Ohio, I first realized that basic, mythical dynamics underlie all interpersonal relationships. I began to see that every society's mythical perspectives link up with fundamental dispositions (archetypes) that aim to root our quest for meaning. Addressing the question of life's meaning is a formidable challenge. Opportunities for real growth lie open to those willing to embark on this adventure. Those who refuse to do so run the risk of drifting into a shallow, meaningless existence.

I invite the reader to search for wisdom by looking deeply into life. This quest will help us understand how group members relate, regardless of whether they are corporate executives, families, or church ministers. The wisdom gleaned during this process will offer insights into our rapidly changing world and suggest ways to deal effectively with social, economic, or personal change. It may give hints as to why we exist at all.

The Search for Meaning provides *common DNA* in our search for meaning, by offering a blueprint that describes the dynamics operative in every person's meaning quest. All of us share this common DNA, which is intimately related to our need to question, communicate on deep mythical levels, ritualize our fundamental beliefs, and find happiness amidst joys and sorrows.

To do this, however, it is necessary for me to share some of my *personal DNA* through autobiographical stories. By reflecting on spiritual aspects of my journey, I hope to offer insights into life's meaning. I feel it necessary to describe my personal search for meaning in order to suggest solid directions for others to pursue in their search for meaning. Years of research, personal experiences, lectures, and feedback from professionals, friends, and students lead me to conclude that this book's approach is a helpful way to proceed.

Many books study meaning, archetype, myth, mythos, ritual, symbol, sign, faith, and models, but few synthesize the dynamics that link them into a coherent perspective. I do this in the succeeding pages.

The Search for Meaning is divided into ten chapters. Chapter 1 situates life's meaning, our need to question, and the human experience of mystery. Chapter 2 considers fundamental assumptions that are necessary for the subsequent analysis of meaning. Chapter 3 looks at core dispositions existing within us, which give basic directions for human life, and chapter 4 concentrates on the societal dynamics underlying our search for meaning.

The remaining chapters look at basic structuring agents in all groups. All human societies are structured at their deepest level by their mythos (myths) and rituals. Mythos refers to a fundamental orientation that establishes the groundwork for a group or individual. It sets the tone for the way we approach life, structure it, and respond in our daily activities. Myths are ways this fundamental orientation is expressed orally, in writing, or by means of technology. Often this happens through stories. Rituals celebrate or act out this fundamental orientation at home, at work, in church, in our neighborhoods, or wherever humans interact.

Chapters 5, 6, and 7 consider mythos and myth, while chapter 8 reflects on rituals. Chapter 9 analyzes symbolic actions and symbols, which find their meaning within the context of mythos and rituals. Finally, chapter 10 reflects on faith as completing our mosaic of meaning. The notes include important, more technical and scholarly clarifications of textual materials.

Throughout these chapters, I will keep the old savings book with me and encourage you to carry your own symbol with you, as we unlock our reasons for being alive.

1

The Old Savings Book:
Mystery and Mythic Meaning

My strong reaction to closing the old savings account involved the deeper meaning of my life. This meaning was not rooted in the $137.38, but came from my bond with Dad. He had opened this account to teach me thrift, but my experience with the savings book reveals three interrelated modes of meaning: secondary, primary, and core mythic meaning.

Secondary mythic meaning can be found in our work and in the meaning we derive from the possession, exchange, or use of material things. My father worked hard for the money he deposited into my account. Most functional activities, such as shoveling snow, washing clothes, or driving an automobile, involve secondary mythic meaning. They are means to the end of maintaining our lives. Often, however, functional actions also relate to a deeper mythic level. This was true in the case of the five dollars that Dad initially deposited in my savings account. Symbolizing his love for me, the money involved more than the currency's face value. So does a parent's work at an unpleasant job to support a family. In such cases, actions normally associated with secondary meaning have deeper meaning.

While planning to close this savings account, I acted as if the $137.38 was of secondary mythic meaning. Upon realizing that it touched a deeper level, I knew why I felt as I did. Then, keeping open the account became the best choice for me. On the other hand, if I needed this money for another, more ultimate reason, such as caring for an aged relative, I may have closed the account, even though ambiguity would be present in this decision.

I experienced *primary mythic meaning* when deciding whether to close the account. Such meaning usually occurs in flesh-and-blood experiences, like my father's and my love, sacrifice, and care. It comes from deep within us and is filtered through memory, imagination, and reason, as we first experience and then later recall beautiful or painful moments. When confronted by primary mythic meaning, we cannot remain neutral. It demands a response.

Many life decisions touch this level of primary mythic meaning. For example, after Dad died, the doctor encouraged Mom to sell her house and move into an apartment. She was visibly upset. His suggestion sent dissonant signals through her. She refused, saying that to leave her home would rip away the roots she needed to continue.

Mom's response came from the context of her primary mythic meaning. Others may have concluded differently. The way each person responds in such circumstances affects the adequacy or inadequacy of one's actions, as they relate to life's meaning.

As in my mother's case, closing the old savings account would have sent dissonant signals through me. When an action demands a primary mythic response, we grow or are frustrated, depending on our decision. From my experience with the old savings book, I concluded that primary mythic meaning is closely related to meaningful actions, resulting from human interactions of a deep kind, usually over a period of time. The pride that we feel in our family or nation comes from this level. It is the realm that indicates the power of cultural responses, like the need of various ethnic communities to maintain their roots, beliefs, and rituals.

Another question surfaces in dealing with meaningful actions, namely, Is there a more fundamental level than primary mythic meaning? Is there a deeper source, linking the primary mythic meaning of what happened with the old account book to similar primary mythic events in other peoples' lives? Is there a similar dynamic underlying every person's search for meaning?

My experience teaches me that the answer to these questions is yes. This most fundamental level is the source of *core mythic meaning,* which is more basic than primary mythic meaning. It is the common inheritance of every person.

Core mythic meaning includes our search to discover meaning that goes beyond money, pleasure, and fame (secondary mythic meaning) to find meaning deeper than the love between a father and son or a wife and husband (primary mythic meaning). Core mythic meaning is the elusive pursuit of answers to life-as-a-whole, such as those relating to birth, death, happiness, and suffering.

Searching for such answers preoccupied me when Dad was near death. During that time, I suffered terribly and so did our entire family. In contrast, I witnessed Mom's joy when we had a surprise party for her on her seventy-fifth birthday. She was overcome with emotion, saying that it was the first surprise birthday party anyone ever had given for her.

All families witness difficult and joyful moments. They are common to every person, because each individual searches for the same core mythic meaning. In this quest we are equals with no distinctions existing between men and women, rich and poor, young and old, black and white. Core mythic meaning enables people of different ages, races, and nationalities to respond in similar ways to life's joys, tragedies, and powerful stories.

Core mythic meaning roots the meaning we find in a friend's love (primary mythic meaning) and the meaning we realize in working for a livelihood (secondary mythic meaning). Questions surfacing from this core mythic level frame our meaning quest and open up levels of reality beyond anything we experience on earth.

Occasionally I toss an old, used brown basketball with a friend. To appreciate its meaning, one must know something

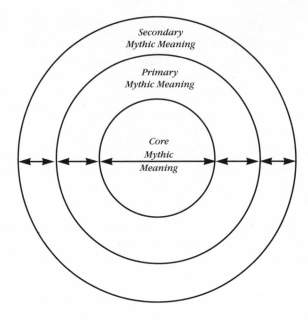

about the ball. My parents gave it to me almost fifty years ago. When I first received the ball, it had secondary mythic meaning. Before then, kids in my neighborhood had no basketball. Now we could play in the school yard.

As this happened, I met new friends, learned to deal with winning and losing and to protect myself from aggressive players. The ball helped me to exercise (secondary mythic meaning), but it also enabled me to relax and enjoy myself, while learning to deal with deeper interpersonal experiences (primary mythic meaning). Often, as I walked home alone after a game, bouncing my ball, I wondered whether there was more to life than winning or losing, going to school, working, and having friends. I thought about God, moral values, life, and death (core mythic meaning).

Today the old basketball has many meanings that were formed during my journey toward adulthood. Every action can be meaningful in different ways, depending on the part it plays in one's life. Viktor Frankl, in *Man's Search for Meaning*, says a person can discover meaning in three ways: doing a deed, experiencing a value, and suffering.[1]

Every day, we *do many deeds* and perform many actions. Such deeds often relate to our work. When carried out to fulfill functional tasks, these actions include secondary mythic meaning, like earning a paycheck.

Some people find little meaning in their jobs but continue working to support a family. Others enjoy their occupations, volunteer to help others, or work around the home to satisfy personal needs (primary mythic meaning).

Work is essential to the human enterprise, and the need to work to find life's meaning is common to every person. Functional work (secondary mythic meaning) receives its deeper meaning and ultimate purpose from primary and core mythical meaning.

Whereas doing a deed requires activity, *experiencing a value* involves receiving more than doing. In this context, we discover meaning by taking a more passive stance. We may experience values while watching a sunset, walking along a wave-beaten seacoast, enjoying a symphony, or receiving another person's love.

These experiences have little to do with secondary mythic meaning but relate directly to primary and core mythic meaning. When experiencing such values, boundaries between primary and core mythic meaning may become blurred. Thus, experiencing a sunset's beauty can inspire us to think about a particular person's beauty or to wonder about the source of beauty itself.

Something similar may happen when we experience another person's love and know that such love is shared each day by different people. Then, we may ask, Where did all this love come from? On such occasions, a profound sense of mystery, flowing from within us, filters into our human experiences. When this happens, the beauty, joy, or love encountered fills us with satisfaction.

Doing deeds and experiencing values, alone, cannot explain the human quest for meaning. They fail to account for human suffering. *Suffering* finds little solace in secondary mythic meaning, rooted in activities. Even primary mythic meaning, based in human relationships, beauty, and truth cannot deal adequately with suffering.

Frankl says that if life has any meaning at all, people must be able to find meaning in suffering.[2] For him, the question is not whether I will suffer. Everyone suffers. Rather, it is whether I find meaning in my suffering. Life without suffering is impossible, but to address life adequately, we must face the challenge of suffering. Suffering forces us to the threshold of mystery. This was made clear to me during my father's last sickness as he lingered near death for months. Dad suffered intensely, unable to breathe properly because of congestive heart failure. This strong, athletic man deteriorated to seventy pounds. He was hardly able to walk or talk. Yet his spirit remained vibrant, and something deeper impelled him to keep struggling. After seeing him, I often pounded my fist on the floor, asking, Why? Why him? He is such a good man. It made no sense.

Years later, I began to find meaning in Dad's suffering. I believe his suffering had something to do with our family. Dad knew that enduring suffering would make it easier for us to accept his death. Today, this realization has tremendous meaning for me. In this way, I found meaning in his suffering.

Suffering takes us to core mythic meaning. Speculation about suffering raises questions that point to an ultimate realm of existence, deeper than we can fathom, which holds the final secret to life's mystery. Experiencing my father's suffering taught me that the search for ultimate meaning is the most fundamental quest on life's journey. The dynamics flowing from questions surrounding core mythic meaning root all primary and secondary mythic responses.

To address the question of meaning is a challenge for the new millennium. Our planet is becoming a more open world, where changing configurations of nations, races, and continents influence the human community. These shifts introduce new perspectives on what it means to be human in a global society.

As this happens, fewer traditional answers are set in stone,

for countries and individuals address the question of meaning in new or different ways. Life-and-death issues, once
decided by religious traditions or churches, are now debated
in the public arena. Such debates are only preludes to more
sophisticated ones to follow, which will challenge society's
moral fiber and force individuals and communities to ask
anew, What is the meaning of life?

In this more open environment, many people address life's
meaning alone or with a few chosen persons. They embark on
this endeavor with fewer constraints from family, religion traditions, or society. Three issues are of particular significance
in dealing with the question of meaning: (1) meaning and
questioning, (2) meaning and community, and (3) meaning as
a lifelong process.

—————————— Meaning in Questioning ——————————

When I felt the emotional surge before closing my old savings
accounts, I asked, Why? The same question surfaced during
my father's suffering. These questions, going beyond rational
analysis, indicate a distinctive human characteristic, namely,
the ability to ask questions. Questioning invites us to address
life issues and clarify them through rational analysis, intuition, and faith.

We ask different kinds of questions. *Functional* ones, involving secondary mythic meaning, are more easily answer-
able but are far less profound. They operate on the rational
level and concern themselves with problem solving—how to
solve a mathematics equation, fix a broken automobile hose,
balance a budget, or operate a computer program.

More *ultimate* questions, involving primary mythic meaning, deal with personal and social relationships. They may
include questions about a person's motives for acting or
motives involved in dealing with a culture different from our
own. Such questions, rarely articulated, can occur the first
time I meet someone. They may include, Will I like this per-

son? What attracts me to him or her? What causes me to with-hold my trust? Ultimate questions arise when we wonder what the future holds or where a particular experience will lead us. A joyful event may move us to gratitude, whereas a painful one may cause us to ask whether we have the courage, determination, or confidence to face it.

Ultimate questions often bring a person face to face with mystery. Such questions, involving primary mythic meaning, push us to delve into core mythic meaning. Profound and difficult to sort out, these questions may include: Why was I born? Why do I suffer? What will happen to me at death? All humans ask these questions, for they spring from core dispositions common to every person. The answers to these questions take different forms, depending on peoples' ages, circumstances, and cultures.

A believer may appeal to faith to answer, Why does my child have to suffer this sickness? A cynic may stress life's absurdity. Regardless of our situation, we need to address such questions to have a meaningful life. Our ability to question is unique on this planet; no other animal operates this way. This key aspect of human life sets us apart from other animals. Questioning is essential to the way we structure our lives, which differs from the way other animals structure their lives. This difference has profound significance in our quest for meaning.

Animal life, excluding humans, is structured primarily from *within* through habit or instinct.[3] The encoding, setting the direction for how these animals live their lives, is found in their genes.

Imagine the scenario of a robin, taken from its nest at birth and raised by swallows in their nest. Even if this robin never sees a robin's nest, when it builds its own nest it builds a robin's, not a swallow's, nest. The robin is genetically structured from within to build a robin's nest from habit or instinct. This does not imply that robins do not learn from experience, but it means that their primary structuring agent is a built-in instinctual response.

Human life, on the other hand, is structured primarily from *without,* through culture, society, community, or family. Imagine another scenario of a human baby, taken at birth from a suburban United States home and raised in a rural African village. After the child matures, he or she will build an African home according to African cultural norms. This indicates society's significance in structuring human values and actions.

Humans also have instincts and habits, but their genetic encoding plays a different role from that of other animals. Human encoding makes it possible for humans to use symbols and develop languages. This ability to use symbols enables humans to form cultures and societies, which are the primary structuring agents in human life. While habit or instinct plays a primary role in how other animals shape their lives, community and society are the strongest influence on human attitudes and ways of acting.

Meaning in Community

All humans ask what will bring happiness. We question within a certain culture, society, family, or group, whose attitudes and values influence us. Many families and societies include "ultimates," such as God, love, deeper quest, or afterlife in their answers. Such ultimate dimensions are found also in contemporary cultures, which increasingly stress functional answers, associated with money, pleasure, material possessions, or sex.

Culture plays a significant role in our search for meaning. I see its importance when I reflect on changes during my lifetime. In my childhood, family life was stable and intergenerational families lived in close geographical proximity. Television sets were rare and computers did not exist. Professional sports were primarily "sports," not business ventures. Life was simpler, and people had more time for one another.

Culture's impact can be seen also in changing attitudes toward authority between my childhood and today. In the 1940s and 1950s, children rarely questioned parental authority, and few adults questioned church or civic authority. We rarely doubted our country's righteousness, as we applauded patriotism. That is not the way things are anymore. Today, our lives are filled with speed, pressure, materialism, and glitz. They shape our attitudes differently from those in the world into which I was born. Living with a foot in both worlds helps me appreciate how past and present social norms influence our attitudes, questions, and pursuit of meaning.

I realized the influence of culture when I participated in the "Native Pastoral Seminar," an Ojibway leadership seminar, in Thunder Bay, Ontario. The sweat-lodge experience, pipe ceremony, and eagle-feather rituals celebrated Ojibway traditions. These people dealt with the same basic questions as I, but in very different ways. Cultural influences were evident, when native women shared their best gifts with the assembled group. One said hers was skinning beavers; another indicated she was best at tanning beaver hides and making moccasins. These natives used their talents to discover meaning in ways far different from most women in the United States.

My time with the Ojibway people confirmed how much a cultural matrix influences the way we fulfill our human potential. Upon returning home and resuming my daily activities, I saw more clearly how we question and search for answers to life issues within a particular meaning system. Such a system includes one's culture, society, family, school, workplace, neighborhood, friends, and other groups. Within a meaning system, as particular as family or as general as culture, we engage in various activities pursuant to our values and goals.[4]

Although cultures differ, the fundamental quest for meaning remains the same. Each culture embeds within itself implicit answers to life's questions. In this process, a culture offers values and modes of action to its members. It also gives them implicit permission to ask some questions and to avoid others. Regardless of our culture, each one includes an intersection of activities involving core, primary, and secondary meaning.

———————————— Meaning in Process ————————————

As I worked on my Ph.D. dissertation, centered on Gordon Allport's theory of the person, a key element eluded me. Put in question form, this item was, What confers unity on my life and holds it together?[5]

I first searched for the answer through academic research. Frustrated in this attempt, I turned to my experience as a teacher, asking what motivated me to enter the teaching profession. This motivation centered on my goal of helping people professionally and personally. To fulfill my responsibilities, I studied, did research, wrote, attended conferences, and prepared classes.

Next I asked myself, What confers unity on this teaching process? Initially I believed the goal itself conferred unity. Soon it became clear, however, that the goal is not enough. When my goal of helping a class learn a particular subject is over at the end of a semester, I must pursue a new goal in relation to a different group of students. This issue remained fuzzy in my mind, so I looked at my personal goals, such as the desire to make a trip to Alaska. To accomplish this, I saved money and studied about the land, and eventually I went there. After the trip was over, this goal was accomplished.

Such experiences caused me to wonder whether the goal itself conferred unity, or did something else? Unable to resolve this issue, I discussed it with my professors. After these conversations failed to pinpoint the source of unity, I wondered if there was an answer. Finally, the answer came in an unexpected way. One afternoon, after a stressful day in class, I returned home exhausted. Unable to concentrate, I took a nap before dinner. In a dream I realized that human values, goals, and activities, taken separately, do not confer unity on life. Rather, *striving to achieve one's goals* confers unity. When a person achieves one goal or changes life's direction, the individual needs to identify new goals or life becomes aimless. With this insight, I realized that my life is unified not by values, goals, or activities in isolation but by striving to achieve my goals in conformity with my value system.

The unity conferred through this process is closely associated with the pursuit of meaning. I saw this in relation to students who switch majors or drop out of school. If meaning depended solely on achieving a goal, what meaning would activities have if one never achieved one's goal? When a person begins college, hoping to become an engineer, but drops out after the first year to support a family, this does not mean that the first year's work had no meaning.

Hence, the proper focus of meaning is not limited to a goal, such as graduating from college or providing food, clothing, and shelter for a family. The same applies to an ultimate religious goal, like heaven for a Christian or nirvana for a Hindu. While such goals give meaning to Christian and Hindu lifestyles, striving to achieve them is included in the search for life's meaning.

This became more evident after I realized that a goal is always in the future, but humans live in the present. Although the full pursuit of meaning includes the goal, actions performed to achieve it are a proper locus of meaning. This became clear during my father's painful last days. During this time, I reflected on the many hours he put into his job to earn a living for our family and on his efforts to make our home clean and nice. These activities afforded him secondary mythic meaning. I also remembered his love for family members, neighbors, and customers, from which he derived primary mythic meaning. This love culminated during his last year, as he endured his suffering to help our family prepare for his death. During his life, Dad put great faith in God. His Christian beliefs afforded him the core mythic meaning that motivated his entire life. In the hospital room, he awaited eternal happiness in the afterlife. The meaning Dad discovered in his final suffering flowed from his values and was directed toward his family-centered goal.

Reflecting on my father's life helped me to understand how striving to achieve our goals includes activities dealing with secondary, primary, and core mythic meaning. We can discover meaning in the sacrifices, joys, and suffering associated with family life. We also find it in tedious labor done for a paycheck, in long hours spent to fulfill graduation requirements, and in volunteer activity.

Working hard, maintaining quality relationships, experiencing beauty, appreciating goodness, feeling sorrow, being faithful to moral standards, affirming cultural roots, and living responsibly are the fiber of life. In them, we discover meaning.

No simple answer exists to the question, What is the meaning of life? A better question is, What is the meaning of my life? A Zen master, when asked about life's meaning, chased away the inquirer with a stick. This was his way of saying that we find life's meaning by living.

2

God's Beautiful Garden: Dimensions of Meaning

After clarifying the dynamics involved in the old savings book story, I saw how different peoples' experiences often connect through their stories. Since the core human story is the same, a common thread connects all stories.

Very tired after a difficult trip, I hoped to relax during the ride from Philadelphia. I sat in the left bulkhead seat next to the aisle. Shortly before take off, the flight attendant seated a four-year-old girl beside me. The last thing I needed was a child gabbing during the entire flight. Instinctively, I slouched down into my seat to avoid conversation. Almost immediately, the child poked my arm and said, "I'm Sue, who are you?" Somewhat startled, I answered, "I'm Bob." "Glad to meet you, Bob," she said. Then, pointing to a rag doll, the child continued, "This is Kim." After greeting Kim, I disappeared further into my seat.

Sue's chattering with Kim caused me to noticed that the child had not buckled her seat belt. I said, "You have to buckle your seat belt." "I don't know how; please buckle it for me," Sue replied. I fastened it and closed my eyes again.

A few moments later, Sue again poked me saying, "You did it wrong, you didn't buckle up Kim." I apologized, as I watched Sue put Kim under her seat belt." After this episode, I started to feel refreshed. Just before the plane left the ground, a voice across the aisle asked me, "Is your name Bob?" After I said yes, the woman continued, "I'm Sarah, and I'm really scared;

this is the first time I've been on a plane. I'm old, handicapped, and can't read or write. Will you buckle me up too?"
So I buckled her up. After the plane was in the air, Sarah
looked toward the window and asked, "Can I take off this belt
and look outside?" I told her to wait until the light went on,
which indicated it was safe to move around the plane. When
this happened a short time later, I said Sarah could go to the
window.

Excitedly, Sarah looked outside and said, "Bob, hurry over
here and see what I see." I did so, and immediately Sarah continued, "What's that, that, that, and that?" pointing to clouds,
hills, rivers, trees, and grass. After I told her what they were,
Sarah looked puzzled and replied in a childlike, humble way,
"No, it's not any of those things." "What is it, then?" I asked.
Sarah said simply, "It's God's beautiful garden." I gulped and
returned to my seat.

Sue, Sarah, and I conversed and laughed the rest of the
trip. When I left them, my fatigue was gone. Upon leaving the
plane, they waved goodbye. At that moment, I knew a deep
part of three very different people touched a common chord,
which sprang from our human oneness. The woman's and
child's simplicity renewed a childlike part of me. Sue's relationship with Kim and Sarah's view of the universe as God's
beautiful garden touched my soul. They opened up dimensions of reality that are discussed under the following head-
ings: meaning and the universe, meaning and mystery,
meaning and the real, and meaning as capable of fulfillment.

Meaning and the Universe[1]

Sarah's words, "It's God's beautiful garden," triggered my
awareness of deeper connections with the universe. Viewed
from the airplane, clouds, trees, rivers, buildings, and people
formed a mosaic embracing a world bigger than me. This perspective helped me understand how human meaning is intimately connected with the universe's meaning.

This episode brought back forgotten memories from the

time I lived in New York. During these years, when walking along Rockaway Beach, I felt swept up into a profound, over-powering, and mysterious reality. The power of waves and wind calmed me and put my problems in better focus. There I was a small actor in a drama larger than myself. The same energies flowing within me pulsated through the wind, waves, and sand.

Here I realized that we must search for meaning within the universe because we are part of it. Oceans, mountains, and the outdoors are our home, as is the place where we sleep. Nature's beauty, majesty, and splendor trigger core mythic meaning, because they resonate with something deep within us. Human society is a key element in this universe. We dis-cover meaning largely through other people and need their support and affirmation to live a fulfilling life. Their love, care, and sacrifice help us maximize our human potential.

While finding meaning in nature and society, we also have responsibility toward them. Consequently, actions on behalf of the universe, society, and other people are part of being human. To discover meaning means living responsibly within the universe. In so doing, we must live in accordance with nature's patterns. They ensure freedom, not take it away.[2] We find meaning only within the context of this freedom.

Responsible freedom operates according to nature's parameters, which set limits on our lives, including what we eat or drink. When we exceed them, we abuse our bodies and jeopardize our health.

People discover core and mythic meaning in conjunction with nature's patterns, not apart from them. Such patterns demand functional work and ultimate experiences, like feel-ing joy, enduring pain, and growing old. They also imply that meaning is found in the life process itself.

Meaning and Mystery

Meaning is framed in mystery. We experience mystery when we stand on a seashore, feel the ocean's power or receive another person's love. Beauty, truth, love, and suffering also bring us to the threshold of mystery, from which core and primary mythic meaning spring. The "Mystery" that frames life breaks open secular rituals that limit themselves to functional activities.

We respond to mystery differently from the way we solve a problem, like repairing a leaky faucet. Secondary mythic meaning, closely associated with functional activities, often includes problem solving. Problems deal with objective, analyzable things or events that require a solution. We have a problem if we lock our car door while the key is inside, or if we are invited to weddings of equally good friends at the same time in different cities. Science, technology, and everyday life require problem solving, as we *objectively* analyze data and offer solutions. So do situations requiring psychological, psychiatric, sociological, and anthropological data.[3]

Mysteries do not work this way, for we are personally involved in a mystery, like love. If we love someone, we are part of the relationship and cannot stand outside of it and offer solutions as we do in problem solving. All experiences of primary and core mythic meaning include mystery.[4]

The difference between problem and mystery becomes clearer when we think of someone we love. A love experience is different from problem solving. Love connects two persons at the depths of their being; it involves a certain communion between people, where their differences become blurred. They may be deeply present to each other, even though separated by space and time. This co-presence helps them overcome the isolation physically separating them. Experiencing such love involves "mystery," incapable of conceptualization, whereas merely talking about love treats it like a problem.

Mystery implies that life is more than than solving problems. On the trip with Sue and Sarah, I felt myself *organically connected* with the air, the clouds, the trees, people, and the plane. Couched in mystery, the whole setting involved more than the sum of its parts. It also embraced energies that keep it in existence and refocus the dynamics of the parts themselves.

Life's meaning is an organic process, not a by-product of a series of linear events or products. Viewing life in "product" terms puts heavy stress on achievements. A person with such an outlook might aim at amassing wealth. What happens when this goal is fulfilled? Will the person try to obtain more wealth? Or will the individual pursue power?

We cannot discover meaning by limiting ourselves to the products of our labors. Success, failure, joy, and sorrow fit into a wider pattern, rooted in how we conform to nature's guidelines in our pursuit of meaning.

Couched in mystery, meaning offers no single road map. It eludes the grasp of any person, philosophy, religion, culture, or life-style. Since cultures, civilizations, and individuals differ, the pursuit of meaning takes various shapes.

Hindus, Buddhists, Muslims, Jews, and Christians interpret core dispositions differently, as they develop their myths, symbols, and rituals. Similarly, Native Americans shape basic attitudes according to their cultural and personal beliefs. So do Africans living in the bush or Inuit peoples struggling near the North Pole. In every instance, a people's quest for meaning meshes with their cultural context to refract a particular life stance. No single way fulfills every person's search for core and primary mythic meaning. Various cultures offer different avenues for us to pursue life's meaning. This realization opens up exciting possibilities for human interactive learning in the new millennium.

Meaning and the Beyond

Human meaning eludes rational analysis. It goes beyond observation, comprehension, and space/time. When Sarah called trees, rivers, clouds, and grass "God's beautiful garden," she poetically reminded me that meaning transcends what we experience in space and time.

Space and time frame all our thoughts.[5] We cannot imagine anything beyond them, like God or heaven, without picturing these notions in space and time. It is impossible, for instance, to envision "heaven" without viewing it somehow in space or time. These categories frame our concepts of God, heaven, or anything that exists beyond perception.

Even though we think in categories of space and time, however, this does not limit what really exists to them. It merely says that human reason needs to use these categories in all its considerations.[6] Ancient mythology and contemporary religions use earthly symbols to picture a transcendent realm beyond the grave. Christian art, ritual, meditation, and theology describe God, heaven, hell, and angels in terms of worldly realities.

Core and primary mythic meaning elude full rational comprehension. I witnessed this during my father's last days. At this time, the universe seemed bigger and life more embracing than the fragile shell of his body. Often I thought, "Life must be more than this. Dad worked hard, loved deeply, and suffered willingly. Will his life end forever in this way?"

Reason afforded no answers. Such reflections, however, helped me understand deeper wellsprings of human personhood, where imagination and insight open up another universe of meaning, and where faith takes over when reason becomes silent.

All major world religions believe that the universe is more than what we perceive. This belief, embedded in the human heart, offers hope during suffering. The transcendent realm of meaning it suggests is more profound than functional categories. The contrast between transcendent meaning and functional categories is apparent in my undergraduate religion courses. At the beginning of each semester, we consider mystery and meaning. Most students find these discussions fascinating, for they rarely think about such issues.

Engineering, business, and science majors are particularly intrigued, for such matters are far removed from their professional training. Some students become disturbed, unable to fit transcendent concepts into their narrowly framed functional categories. Others become excited, for this perspective opens them up to a challenging new world. They see "mystery" as an opportunity to search openly for the transcendent. In this venture, they get a glimpse into why they are alive.

Experiencing Native American religious rituals helped me appreciate this quest for the transcendent. Such rituals reflect the belief that life's meaning embraces more than we comprehend. We are rooted in the earth, which is our mother. Since all creation participates in the earth story, humans, animals and plants are brothers and sisters, and the wind, the sun, and the moon influence us in real ways.

They celebrate such beliefs in sweat-lodge rituals. Before one such celebration, an elder told me, "We enter the lodge on our hands and knees. It is done this way out of reverence, because we are entering mother earth's womb." As he spoke, I wondered if Native Americans *literally believe* that the sweat lodge is mother earth. Later, a woman gave me the answer when we were discussing an Ojibway creation story of how turtle island, their name for the Americas, was formed. The story says that sky woman invited several animals to swim to the water's bottom to get some earth. After they failed, the muskrat offered to try. He succeeded, bringing wet mud to the surface, even though he gave up his life to do it. From the mud, turtle island was created.

I asked the native woman if she believed that this myth is literally true. Puzzled, she replied, "What difference does it make? The story is true and real. It matters little whether it is literally true or not?" I never before thought of truth and reality in such terms. Previously, I believed myths had deep meaning, but described them as not literally true. Consequently, I taught creation stories, including the Seven-Day and Adam-and-Eve creation accounts in Genesis, in terms of literal and nonliteral truth (see Genesis 1:1–2:4 and 2:5ff.).

Her words about "truth" (the real) and "literal truth" changed my focus. The deeper meaning of truth is most fully associated with the real and is not limited to literal truth. Her words also deepened my appreciation of connections between core, primary, and secondary mythic meaning. The first two are the realm of "truth" or the "real," while the third is the realm of "literal truth," only one aspect of the real.

With this insight, I understand better what the sweat lodge means to Native Americans. For them, it matters little if crawling into the sweat lodge is literally entering the womb of mother earth. Their meaning structure embraces a truth, deeper-than-literal truth, which finds core mythic meaning in the connection between humans and the earth. Their beliefs also find primary mythic meaning through the links established between those celebrating this ritual. Finally, common patterns in the sweat-lodge ritual—it is celebrated somewhat differently from place to place—bring comfort to the participants. They find secondary mythic meaning in such functional patterns.

Ojibway belief systems confirm Viktor Frankl's words: "Logos is deeper than logic."[7] By this he means that life's ultimate meaning eludes logical analysis. A transcendent realm grounds our place in the universe. Here we find meaning when our actions are in harmony with life's rhythms.

Before dealing with Native Americans, I studied their rituals and beliefs, which were far removed from my world. When exposed to their stories and rituals, I realized that their beliefs connect with a deep dimension of my inner self. After this happened, I often wondered, Which world is more real, theirs or mine? With this question before me, I am less inclined to look for differences in peoples' worldviews and more likely to see a common core reality in all cultures.[8]

Core Native American beliefs say that more exists than we put into categories. This awareness presumes a reality beyond space and time and points toward the transcendent. It also invites us to develop a new openness to various life possibilities. Such an openness begins in our childhood, when we enter life with trust and enthusiasm. Over time, disappointment, rejection, and hurt temper our optimism. Experiences like those with Native American people invite us to rediscover an openness that easily can be forgotten in our journey to maturity. In this way we can renew our faith in nature's harmonious laws, which ground existence. Seen holistically, these laws energize the universe, stabilize its parts, and influence every creature. Since we are nature's children, she takes care of us. In turn, we are responsible for her well-being. Such an openness to a greater cosmic whole focuses life's meaning.

Native American core beliefs surrounding what is real often contrast with those found, for example, in many television programs which associate the "real" with materialistic values and with what satisfies the senses. Such programs show little regard for values related to primary and core mythic meaning. Rather, they limit themselves to secondary mythic meaning. When watching them, I sometimes ask, "Is this all there is?"[9]

This question challenges us to acknowledge that life's deepest realities come from a realm of existence that is steeped in mystery. We appreciate this life dimension more as we learn from one another and from other religious traditions. This exciting learning possibility awaits us in the new millennium.

──────── Meaning, Religion, and the Real ────────

People's backgrounds and worldviews significantly influence their attitude toward religion. *Religion* is every person's search for life's ultimate meaning.[10] This search includes the deeper quest for core and primary mythic meaning.

Religion touches a profound dimension of the human person. It extends beyond merely belonging to or going to church. It crosses personal and denominational lines. Some non-churchgoing individuals may be considered religious if they believe and relate to their God, while showing love, compassion, and concern for people. On the other hand, church members with little regard for core and primary mythic values are hardly considered religious.

Religion is connected with becoming a mature person.[11]

This begins at conception and lasts a lifetime. Three dimensions of the process lead to mature religion, namely, outreach to life, knowing oneself, and integrated life stance.[12] *Outreach to life,* or the need to reach beyond oneself, is a necessary part of human development.[13] When a child reaches out to a parent for comfort, a student to a teacher for help, or a parent to a friend for advice, the response each individual receives shapes the individual's subsequent outlook.

As a child, I received loving, supportive responses from my parents. When sickness kept me home from school in the first grade, Mom taught me. During adolescence, Dad's store provided a wonderful work environment. There I learned to communicate with customers in ways that influenced my subsequent dealings with people.

To satisfy the human search for meaning, an outreach to life necessitates more than bodily gratification in the way of food, clothing, sex, or comfort. It involves seeking deeper levels of fulfillment, often associated with beauty, love, truth, aesthetic values, and ethical responses. Without such inner movements one's life and search for meaning remain narrow and dwarfed.

Through outreach to life, I developed a positive image of myself. A critical aspect of becoming a mature person is forming an opinion of oneself that mirrors who one is and how others see one. This process can be called *knowing oneself.*

Positive experiences of love at home, in school, and at the store helped me to acknowledge my gifts and admit my weaknesses. Along the way, clashes with neighborhood kids, school disappointments, failures at sports, and bickering with brother and sisters added to my growing self-perception.

While outreach to life takes us outside ourselves, knowing oneself brings us back within ourselves. As this happens, a mature person gradually develops an *integrated life stance* that provides overall direction and consistency to our values, goals, and actions.

People develop different life stances, which may be aesthetic, ethical, social, economic, political, or religious. One

individual unifies his or her activities around a social perspective, which focuses the person's goals and actions on
concern for others. Another concentrates on money or material success (economic) to give direction to life. A third
embraces a leadership career, centering on power in government, church, or business (political). A fourth dedicates
attention to artistic enterprises. (aesthetic). Yet another one
weaves the best of each previous philosophy into an overall
synthesis (religious).[14]

If a single life stance dominates a person's activities, it
becomes the master motive for action. It is rare, however, that
one such perspective predominates to the exclusion of the
rest. Usually, two or three interact to direct a person's life.
Seen holistically, a mature religious orientation is the most
embracive of all, for it excludes nothing worthwhile from its
interests.[15] It is dynamic, consistently directive, comprehen-
sive, open, and flexible. When mature religion is a person's
master motive, it gives unity and purpose to one's values,
goals, and actions.[16]

A mature religious person operates in the real world and
finds meaning by probing beyond secondary mythic meaning
to core and ultimate meaning. This individual knows that
meaning includes complex realities associated with right living, work, transcendence, social concerns, functional responsibilities, beauty, truth, and goodness. Such a person sees
functional activities as means to achieve deeper values.

Meaning and Fulfillment

Orderly patterns exist in nature. Each December, as we sit in
our kitchen, Mom looks out the back window and says, "On
December 27th, the sun sets over the doctor's home on the far
hill. Then, it slowly moves in an easterly direction and the
days get longer." Before Dad died, he sat by this same window
and described how crows in the adjacent field change behavior before a snowstorm.

I own a small section of Indiana forest land, which manifests nature's regular patterns. When a United States conservationist established a plan for the land, he said, "If you leave this barren field alone, it will reforest itself. First grass comes, then thorns and thistles. After they cool the land by tempering the sun's heat, shrubs and bushes grow. Then, softwood trees spring up, and finally, hardwoods appear. In this way, a mature hardwood forest will develop in about a hundred years." The land reforests itself because the universe is an interconnected organic unity.[17] Each rock, plant, and animal influences the whole. Without such order, the planet would fall into ruins. Nature's order enables science to predict natural events, medicine to cure patients, and technology to form global telecommunication networks. Regularity in the universe makes life possible.

Governed by the universe's laws, we question, analyze, and set directions in ways not possible to other creatures. Patterns analogous to those found throughout nature regulate human actions and ground our search for meaning. In this context two questions surface: What natural patterns root our desire for ultimate meaning? What patterns exist within us from which the meaning quest springs?

To address these questions, it helps to contrast human responses and those of other animals. Well-developed *instincts* enable birds, fish, reptiles, and animals to survive. They dictate the direction their activities take.

Five years ago, I witnessed Alaskan salmon migrating up the Russian River to their destination, returning to the exact location where they were born. Here, female salmon spawn a new generation and the adults die. After the eggs hatch, the newborn salmon are pulled backward by the current down the same river into the sea, where they disappear into ocean's depths. Eventually, they return to this river as mature, strong adults, ready to fight currents, rapids, and fishing enthusiasts in their journey to their place of origin. After laying their eggs, they die near the place they were born.

The cycle continues, generation after generation, ordered

by instincts within every salmon. Such built-in directions, which are blueprints for each animal species, exist for a purpose. Nature does not establish them without the possibility of their fulfillment.

Core dispositions are dynamic patterns existing in every person that can lead us to fulfillment as humans. These inborn dispositions set the tone for our search for meaning and hint at a life that does not end at death. These dispositions, analogous to animal instincts, give direction to the human search for meaning. Existing at the depths of our personhood, they move us to ask, Who am I? Where did I come from? Why is there suffering? How do I find happiness? and What happens after death? They challenge us to search for life's meaning.

Most people believe that life continues beyond the grave. From the beginning of the human race, pictographic records, written accounts, and oral traditions confirm this belief. If nothing existed beyond this world to fulfill the aspiration to live on after death, the patterned order found throughout nature would break down in human beings. Nothing else in the universe indicates such failure. A moth larva cannot realize its fulfillment as a butterfly while still a larva. This does not mean that the moth does not eventually become a butterfly. A fish under water never sees the sun except through reflected rays. This does not mean that the sun does not exist outside the water. Just as the fish sees the sun through water, so humans perceive life's meaning through worldly categories. Like the butterfly larva, humans cannot appreciate their ultimate destiny during earthly existence.

Nature's patterned activities indicate strong possibilities that humans can fulfill their desire for meaning. Every major religious tradition draws this conclusion. This built-in need for fulfillment points humans in a direction beyond space and time. The eternal "hope for more" is no accident; it invites ultimate realization.

Core dispositions, part of nature's plan, set directions for life. As other animals relate to their world, so humans relate to the earth community in order to fulfill their destiny, which is never realized fully in this life. A loving relationship partially fulfills the human desire for core and primary mythic meaning. Such lasting love overcomes separateness, diminishes loneliness, and alleviates fear. A sunset's beauty or a walk in the forest also may address such deep yearnings.

Such experiences hint at a life beyond the earth, where human aspirations reach ultimate realization. The universe's orderly patterns afford hope that the human quest for meaning will be realized. Achieving it depends on how people's activities mesh with the basic yearnings of the human heart.

When secular culture addresses happiness, suffering, and death, it often gives answers pertaining to secondary, not primary and core mythic meaning. We cannot satisfy our deep needs by limiting ourselves to secondary mythic meaning, when our questions come from the core level. A student reminded me of this point.

Karen's assignments often spoke sadly about her father, a successful attorney. In her youth, she rarely saw him, even at school plays, sports activities, or dance recitals. She justified his absence by saying he was busy with his business. After class, Karen said, "He showed his care by paying for my education and giving me material things, including a new convertible, when I was sixteen." Then, sadly she concluded, "He gave me everything but what I really wanted. I wanted him to spend time with me—to laugh, cry, and play. I wanted his love, but he gave me things."

Deep human needs reflect core dispositions that yearn for fulfillment. Karen's father failed to appreciate her real needs. Her sadness resulted from an inability to find primary and core mythic meaning in their relationship. The things he gave Karen never satisfied her.

3

Nostalgia for Paradise: Meaning—Connecting at the Core

The old savings book did more than connect me with a forgotten memory of the day Dad and I first entered the Glenway Loan and Deposit Company. It symbolized a complex web of relationships between us, including birth, growing up, sports, vacations, work, suffering, and death. It had a deep primary mythic meaning, because my father was my hero.

Dad never finished high school. At sixteen he went to work in his father's small dry goods store to help support eight brothers and sisters. Through his half-century of work there, he supported our family and gave us educational opportunities he did not enjoy.

By reminding me of his life, the old book inspired me to look deeper into my own life. I am alive, Dad is dead; but our love continues. What is it that allows love to transcend even death itself? Questions like this intensified during the Ojibway Leadership Conference, especially after I met Lucy. The first night of the conference I noticed a middle-aged woman in a wheelchair. She wore braces on her wrists and feet. My immediate thought was, "Why is this handicapped woman at a leadership conference? She is unable to control her movements." Later I learned her name was Lucy. The next day a Native American woman read poetry that Lucy had written. The assembly listened respectfully to her wise words. I began to understand why she was there. Moreover, I learned that

Native American traditions hold that handicapped people like Lucy possess unique abilities to share deep mysteries of life.

Lucy and I became friends. We discussed various issues, especially her poetic gifts. Lucy's vibrant spirit emanated from a handicapped body, much the same way that Dad's spirit poured from his fragile body shortly before his death.

Experiencing their spirits help me to appreciate the depths of human personhood. This chapter probes further into the question of meaning in relation to enfleshing the spirit, connecting at the core, and linking with society and the universe.

Enfleshing the Spirit

Experiences like those with Dad and Lucy led me to describe the human person as an *enfleshed spirit*.[1] We are spirits-in-flesh. "Enfleshed" indicates our rootedness in this planet. "Spirit" indicates a deeper dimension within us that goes beyond the limits that confine our earthly bodies to this place or time.

Dad was an enfleshed spirit; his spirit remained vibrant, even when he was dying. His body deteriorated, but his spirit never wavered.[2] After his death, our love goes on, as our spirits continue to touch. Lucy's body is severely handicapped, but her spirit is alive. We remain joined in spirit, even though hundreds of miles separate us.

As *enfleshed*, we pursue meaning in this world, which is our home. We come from the earth, and here we work out our destiny. As *spirits*, we strive to satisfy our spiritual selves, which transcend earthly existence. As *enfleshed spirits*, we experience love, beauty, and hope, and we communicate with God through prayer.

After Viktor Frankl's separation from his wife in the concentration camp, he describes a continued relationship with her. In a moving passage, Frankl says that love for her was not conditioned upon whether she was alive or dead. He says:

> My mind still clung to the image of my wife. . . . I didn't even

know if she were still alive. I knew only one thing. . . . Love
goes very far beyond the physical person of the beloved. It finds
its deepest meaning in his spiritual self, his inner being.
Whether or not he is actually present, whether or not he is still
alive at all, ceases somehow to be of importance.

There was no need for me to know; nothing could touch the
strength of my love, my thoughts, my image of my beloved.[3]

Religious traditions acknowledge this spiritual dimension
of the human person. It roots the Hindu belief in reincarnation and the Jewish belief that Yahweh-God "breathed into
"his nostrils a breath of life, and thus man became a living
being" (Genesis 2:7). Judaism believes this "breath" is God's
spirit.

Christians often relate this spiritual dimension to the
"soul," and Christianity teaches that humans do not exist
prior to birth. During life they are enfleshed spirits; after
death their spirits continue, still connected in some way with
the earth.

As enfleshed spirits, people are challenged to balance the
flesh and spirit dimensions. The spiritual self roots core questions, such as Why was I born? What is the meaning of life?
and What happens after death?

———————— Connecting at the Core ————————

Before I left the Ojibway Leadership Seminar, Lucy asked me
and a friend to visit her home. I willingly accepted this invitation. Lucy lived in a simple two-room apartment. After our
arrival, she showed us volumes of her poems and other works
containing Native American stories, wisdom, and traditions. I
asked how she wrote them, since she was unable to control
her movements. Lucy showed me an old computer. With a
stick, she punched out each word, letter by letter, to compose
her works. Beauty radiated from this simple woman, who was
unable to stand or walk and barely able to talk. Lucy gave me
a small book she had written, which described her childhood

in the northern Canadian bush. In it, Lucy told of bluebells, fish, cold days, warm sun, and the water she fetched from the lake.

Near the end of our visit, Lucy reflected on the days, weeks, and months that she sat alone, looking out her window at a tree. I asked if the tree communicated with her. She said, "Yes. Through it I hear God's voice speaking of life." Finally, she inquired, "Will I ever see you again?" I answered, "If I can, someday, I will return."

Common core dispositions enable people to connect on deep levels. Such dispositions manifest themselves in experiences like those I shared with Lucy. Poetry, music, philosophy, and mythology also reflect their presence.[4]

Core dispositions are inner and dynamic directions common to all people, which move us to actualize our unique potential as humans in relation to a set of fundamental connections on which the universe is based.[5]

Core Dispositions move us to *search in similar directions* during life. All humans desire fulfillment, unity, love, happiness, and roots. I cannot explain what moved me to accept Lucy's invitation to visit her home, but it was not merely to make her feel good. Somehow this visit also fulfilled a deep need in me. The spiritual bond that emerged between us during the Ojibway Leadership Seminar is not explainable by reason. Ellie's invitation and my response came from dispositions deep within us.

Human tendencies flowing from core dispositions are more fundamental than is food for our fulfillment as persons. Eating satisfies a biological need and is necessary for bodily survival; but love actualizes a spiritual need and is necessary for personal fulfillment. Lucy's loving concern and her description of God's love, experienced through the tree outside her window, struck a spiritual chord within me.

Such inner and dynamic movements originate within us as aspects of our spiritual selves. Just as instincts give inner direction to animals, helping them to fulfill their animal potential, so core dispositions give *inner direction* to humans, helping them to fulfill their human potential.[6]

These active, structuring principles suggest a road map for the way that humans question, address issues, and respond to life. They offer flexible directions that invite us to question on an ultimate level. They moved me to question Lucy about life.

All humans respond to the same core dispositions. They provide the dynamism that allows people to discover core and primary mythic meaning. In different ways, these dispositions establish foundations for family solidarity, social involvement, group cohesion, and patriotism. Core dispositions move humans to actualize their unique potential in relation to a *set of fundamental connections,* on which the universe is based. They offer guidance during life's journey, move us to overcome isolation, encourage us to reach out to others, and invite us to search beyond money and pleasure to fulfill ourselves as persons. This happened with Lucy and me.

We actualize core dispositions by acting in accordance with the directions they suggest. There is, however, no single determined path for every person to follow. Core dispositions are flexible, allowing many variations, as people strive to actualize them. They urge us to ask questions relating to core mythic meaning, such as Where did I come from? and move us to answer them in an ultimate, not a functional, way. The answers given, however, are affected by religious traditions and cultures. An orthodox Hindu, steeped in a caste system, explains human origins differently than does an orthodox Jew, who believes in one God. In other words, energies from core dispositions, which incline people to ask ultimate questions, concretize themselves in the myths, symbols, and ritual activities of various cultures.

Core dispositions challenge us to search for meaning. They move us toward wholeness and deep connections with others, which provide primary mythic meaning. They cry out for actualization, as we strive to overcome loneliness, meet new friends, or find a spouse. They challenge us to keep in balance those activities associated with secondary mythic meaning. Moving us to wonder about old age and death, they seek fulfillment beyond earthly existence.[7]

An altruistic activity or a powerful experience, story, or event elicits strong emotion because it connects with a core disposition. One such experience happened during Dad's final sickness. The second evening Dad was in the hospital, a heart specialist arrived. After examining my father, he called me into the corridor and said bluntly, "He will not recover." This stunned me, and I replied, "What can be done to help him?" "Nothing," the doctor said. "He may live a day, a week, or a month, but his time is definitely limited." I went to the car, sat down, and sobbed. The realization that my Dad was dying struck something deep within me.

Core dispositions, flowing from the spiritual core of our corporeal body, have not changed since the beginning of the human race. Some religious traditions associate the spiritual self, from which they come, with the soul.[8] Analogous to electricity in a material realm, core dispositions offer spiritual urges that provide light and direction in the human search for meaning.

Revealing a transcendent dimension of human becoming, core dispositions move us toward realizable satisfaction on earth and ultimate fulfillment beyond space and time. Various world religions refer to such fulfillment in terms of union with God, nirvana, heaven, and a happy hunting ground.

Core dispositions resemble Carl Jung's *archetypes* or *archetypal patterns,* which he considers inner patterns of human response. Jung describes archetypes as dynamic factors in our personality. These primordial images, present in the collective unconscious of the human race, are found in myths, religion, dreams, fantasies, and literature.[9] Their origins are unknown, but they are repeated in different, unconnected peoples and places. Archetypes possess considerable meaning, power, energy, and initiative that affect our lives.[10]

Core dispositions differ from Jung's archetypes in reference to their origins. Core dispositions, rooted within each person, were given to the human race from the beginning. They did not change because of humankind's past history. Jung's archetypes, on the other hand, include primordial memories of the past, contained in the human race's collective unconscious.

Similarities in myths, religion, dreams, fantasies, and literature are often seen in stories of a flood, hero, or savior god. These similarities make sense, because common core dispositions mesh with different cultural experiences of birth, tragedy, suffering, and death. There are also differences in myths that reflect cultural differences between the peoples who developed them. Although the local coloring of myths, stories, or rituals varies, their underlying dynamism results from common core dispositions.[11]

Core dispositions invite people to live a balanced life by keeping activities associated with core, primary, and secondary mythic meaning in proper focus. As enfleshed spirits, we need to balance life's functional and ultimate dimensions to ensure stability and growth. Core dispositions move us on a regular yet flexible path into the future by offering the basic directions needed to complete ourselves as persons.

People are connected through core dispositions. Common needs for unity, wholeness, justice, happiness, love, hope, and ultimate fulfillment draw us together for support, knowledge, love, and wisdom. Our search for core mythic meaning is central to the human quest, in spite of cultural variations, sexual differences, age, and socioeconomic status.

Creation myths grow up around a given society's fundamental beliefs. These myths implicitly reveal basic core dispositions that give direction to the quest for meaning, happiness, and fulfillment. Sometimes creation stories are referred to as "Nostalgia-for-Paradise" myths, thereby indicating a built-in desire for happiness.[12] They describe a deep dynamism flowing from core dispositions—namely, the common desire for fulfillment.[13] These myths acknowledge human limitations and look beyond this earth to a transcendent realm, associated with God, gods, or spiritual beings.

They consider suffering, death, and struggle as connected with the earth's origins.

The Hebrew Bible begins with two separate creation stories. The *Seven-Day creation story* addresses the good existing in the world. It describes creation as God's handiwork and sees humans as made in God's (*Elohim's*) image. This myth challenges us to act responsibly in the world that comes from God's hands (Genesis 1:1–2; 3).[14]

The *Adam-and-Eve creation story* addresses the issues of evil, death, and unhappiness, which are the results of a fall from grace with Yahweh God (Genesis 2:4ff.). This paradise myth reflects a core disposition moving humans toward happiness, which is closely associated with overcoming sin. This myth teaches that after the fall of Adam and Eve, humans need to work. It also contains an implicit "messianic hope," hinting at future redemption for Yahweh's faithful people.[15]

An Apache myth contains some themes that are similar to those found in the Adam-and-Eve account in Genesis. The Native American story describes human origins in terms of God, earth, and Dog. It begins with the Creator walking around with Dog. God tells Dog that some day God may have to live far away. Then Dog asks the Creator to make him a companion. A human being is formed as the Creator lies on the earth, while Dog draws an image around the great Creator. The Creator tells the Human to sit, stand, speak, and laugh. After the Human does all these things, the Creator says that the Human is now fit to live. The myth concludes on a sad note, as the Human leaves the Creator and goes off with Dog.[16]

Central to this story is the Apache belief that the Creator never leaves humans, but when we get too involved with created things, God often is given a back seat. Lack of fulfillment occurs when we become preoccupied with created things, thereby failing to recognize God's abiding presence.

Hindu mythology contains many creation myths, each manifesting aspects of the human search for fulfillment. The *Rig Veda* contains a myth of the sacrifice of the Primal Man, which sets the stage for the caste system. In the myth, all creation, including plants, animals, and human social classes, emerged from one quarter of the sacrificed body of Parusha (the Primal Human). The remaining three-quarters is indescribable and transcendent.[17] This myth indicates that each caste is predetermined. Every Hindu's ultimate destiny depends on patterns implied in this myth.

Besides mythological evidence, experience points to the universal desire for meaning and fulfillment.[18] Although humans search for happiness in love, even intimate love experiences never fully satisfy them. Mature love partially satisfies a deep yearning coming from core dispositions. Maternal, paternal, filial, altruistic, and marital love point toward happiness that transcends earthly experience. No matter how good people feel about family, work, friends or accomplishments, these cannot satisfy their search for meaning. Centuries ago, Augustine pointed to the need for "something more" in these words: "For thou hast made us for thyself and restless is our heart until it comes to rest in thee."[19]

——Linking with Society and the Universe——

Patterns existing throughout the universe allow core dispositions to mesh with the wider world. Core dispositions, giving general direction to the search for meaning are the "within" of the quest. The external world, including the various groups in which people live and work are the "without" of their quest. To discover meaning, a complementary relationship must exist between the directions from within and the without of the external world of beliefs, actions, and structures.

When a person's core need for love is reciprocated by deep experiences of human love, this core disposition is on the road to actualization. On the other hand, when this need is met with rejection or a materialistic substitute for real love, alienation often results. Each individual is part of a larger meaning system, including one's family, friends, work associates, neighbors, church, city, state, nation, planet, and universe. We begin our earthly journey in a human family, part of the broader society. Society, in turn, is part of the earth community, which is part of the universe. This organic unity contains patterns that enable us to actualize the general movements given through core dispositions.

For one elderly Native American, experiencing the sunset satisfied a movement coming from a core disposition, present in his spiritual self.

> Sam watched the sunset every evening in the rear of his home, transfixed by its beauty. He encouraged his children to sit and watch it with him. "When my brothers and sisters reached adolescence," his daughter recounted, "we preferred to watch television or play games instead." This disturbed my father, who often said, " How can you do such trivial things at this time? Do you not appreciate the great miracle that happens every evening right before our eyes?"

Sam realized that the universe contains within itself ways to experience meaning, beauty, truth, goodness, love, and happiness.

4

A Whimpering Child:
Society and the Quest for Meaning

The story of the savings book illustrates how childhood experiences leave an imprint on adult life. Many external factors influenced my attitudes, feelings, and actions as I grew to maturity. No single way exists for every person to deal with life events.

Core dispositions (the "within" of personal development) are actualized in contact with the external world (the "without"). The world, especially human society, is the primary structuring agent in human becoming.[1]

Edie, a church worker, was making her rounds in a rundown tenement house, when she heard whimpering behind a closed door. Thinking a dog was injured, she knocked. After no one answered, she entered the unlocked door.

The whimpering intensified, as Edie walked into a back room. There she saw a two-foot wooden post nailed to the floor with a four-foot rope attached to it. Some uneaten food lay around the post. A girl's hands were tied to the other end of the rope. The child grunted, whimpered, and ran around the post like an animal.

Fearing for the girl's safety, Edie took her to a social service agency. The police waited at the apartment for the return of whoever tied up the child. After the girl's parents returned home, they admitted to tying her up. They were taken to the social agency where the child was held. Upon seeing her parents, the girl ran to them. They embraced and expressed deep love and affection.

As this was happening, the church worker saw that the child's parents were very mentally handicapped. Married some years ago, they had had two previous children, who were removed from their home by the social agency. When the woman got pregnant the third time, the parents told no one about their child. They loved and protected her the best way they could.

After psychological testing, it was learned that the child was born with normal intelligence. Because of severe circumstances of her upbringing, she would never function as a normal person. Even though her parents showed the girl love, she could not make up for what she had missed. After nine months, the child could speak only a few words.

This child's life was structured primarily from "without" by the parents who raised her. The girl's growth process, which needed actualization in quasi-normal social relations, was severely impeded. This early situation influenced the rest of her life.

The "without," which actualizes our human potential, includes various dimensions of the external world. A sunset's beauty, a tornado's power, or an ocean's vastness influences us. So do healthy family settings or dysfunctional homes, because core dispositions need adequate relationships with the outside world to actualize their potential.

This chapter looks at interactive patterns between humans and their world. It considers open and closed societies, ultimate and functional dimensions, and human response modes. It also introduces the notions of mythos and rituals. These fundamental dynamics structure our lives.

Open and Closed Societies

Individuals, families, clubs, businesses, nations, and religious organizations interact with groups beyond their environments. Some have more contact with outside groups than others.

When I was young, the world beyond my family was limited to neighbors, friends, and church. Except for a yearly vacation and a Sunday automobile ride, I rarely went more than three blocks from home. Television did not exist, and I learned the news from papers, radio, and word of mouth. I grew up in a relatively closed society.

Today, people move often; children attend schools beyond their immediate neighborhood; mothers and fathers work; and parents leave town regularly on business. Television, videos, and computers introduce people to a broader world. Mobility separates intergenerational families and brings ethnic diversity into every community. Nations are becoming a global society. People are increasingly skeptical of institutions, and churches enjoy less authority. Contemporary society is a relatively open one.

Societies are *closed* or *open,* depending on their degree of reciprocity with individuals, groups, and viewpoints different from theirs. No society is completely closed or open. Every family, organization, or church falls somewhere between a relatively closed and a relatively open society. A *relatively closed society* has little significant contact with outside groups. Its energy is expended largely within the group itself, and strong dynamics control its members' actions.[2]

My childhood family lived in a relatively closed society. Some contact existed with the outside world, but for the most part, we rarely lived, worked, and played with people of different religious, social, economic, and ethnic backgrounds. Our neighborhood's narrowly confined dynamics structured our basic life patterns.

A *relatively open society* allows a freer energy flow between individuals and groups. In this open encounter, different ways of acting influence each other. Today's families are more open than were families in my childhood. Parents and children are more inclined to question, probe, and challenge. Although family rules still exist, children are freer within them.

Changing attitudes toward women encourage mothers to work beyond the home. This openness was not present years ago. My fourth-grade teacher said, "Boys, not girls, have logical minds and make good mathematicians. Girls are too emotional." Ironically, my sister earned her Ph.D. in mathematics, while I earned mine in philosophy.

A society's openness also applies to countries. Until communism collapsed in Eastern Europe and Russia, these nations were relatively closed societies, which gave few freedoms to their citizens. This contrasted with relatively open attitudes in the United States, Western Europe, Canada, and Japan. Today, people in former communist bloc countries struggle with their new-found freedom, as they assume the democratic way.[3]

Dynamics operative within closed and open societies play a role in the way people develop attitudes and structure their lives. In a closed society, the message is, "This is the way it is—accept it." This is reflected in one woman's experience soon after she arrived in the United States from a totalitarian country. She went to a shopping mall, and a neighbor bought a small transistor radio. As they left the store, the neighbor took it from the bag and gave it to her. Looking about nervously, she said, "Put it away." When he asked why, she replied, "If the police see it, they will take it, and I won't have it anymore." Her reaction came from past experiences in her country, where the police regularly confiscated such items.

People often fail to understand how a society's openness or closedness affects their search for meaning. They appreciate this better when they compare patterns of their childhood with present practices in schools, businesses, governments, churches, and neighborhoods.

Ultimate and Functional Dimensions

All societies include ultimate dimensions, like love, play, and prayer, and functional ones, like typing, writing, and cutting grass. The *ultimate* is the focus of core and primary mythic meaning, whereas the *functional* is the realm of secondary mythic meaning. These flow into one another like a both/and. The following schema illustrates their relationship.

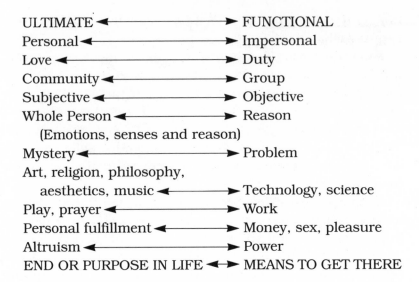

ULTIMATE ←——————————→ FUNCTIONAL
Personal ←——————————→ Impersonal
Love ←——————————→ Duty
Community ←——————————→ Group
Subjective ←——————————→ Objective
Whole Person ←——————————→ Reason
   (Emotions, senses and reason)
Mystery ←——————————→ Problem
Art, religion, philosophy,
   aesthetics, music ←——————————→ Technology, science
Play, prayer ←——————————→ Work
Personal fulfillment ←——————————→ Money, sex, pleasure
Altruism ←——————————→ Power
END OR PURPOSE IN LIFE ←——→ MEANS TO GET THERE

The ultimate involves *personal* experiences, like love, kindness, and sacrifice. *Impersonal* actions, like typing or driving, are functional.

Whereas *love* is ultimate, *duty* is functional. Many people fulfill job commitments in a functional way. Such work, carried out to satisfy a sense of duty, is necessary in any society.[4]

Community includes a dimension of ultimacy and involves warmer, more intimate feelings than are associated with a *group.* The latter is often functional, like a mathematics class, organizational meeting, or work force. Such groups are not communities.[5] Consequently, all communities are groups, but not all groups are communities.

The ultimate pertains to the *subjective,* whereas functional activities are *objective.* Love embraces a person's subjective side, which cannot be fully analyzed by objective, measurable norms. Using a computer requires objective precision to carry out its functions.

An ultimate experience involves the *whole person.* The joy felt on a special anniversary is deeper than memory, reason, and emotions taken separately. Our whole person is caught up in the happiness of such a moment. On the other hand, we rely on *reason* to probe facts in mathematics, business and everyday life.

The ultimate springs from the realm of *mystery*, whereas the functional deals with *problem solving.* Human love involves mystery too deep to analyze. We are embraced by a mystery, like love. Since we are part of it, we cannot view it objectively from the outside. On the other hand, we can stand outside a problem and analyze it objectively to get a solution. If we have knowledge and skills, we can solve a problem, like repairing a broken fence.

Art, religion, philosophy, and *music* pertain to the ultimate, whereas *science and technology* concern themselves with the functional. Teaching philosophy to science majors often elicits different orientations from those of students pursuing liberal arts degrees. The latter may find it harder to think scientifically, whereas the former often experience difficulty in dealing with the realm of mystery.

Play and *prayer* raise us above the confines of space–time and thrust us into an ultimate realm. *Play* is ultimate, for it goes beyond competitive demands of game playing. Professional sports are games, not play. When money or profit is the bottom line, it rarely includes much real play. *Prayer* also breaks the bonds of space–time, by moving us toward an ultimate realm. In contrast to play and prayer, *work* is functional. It is limited to space–time, as a necessary part of human survival, progress, and growth.

The ultimate leads us to *personal fulfillment.* Here, core and primary dispositions achieve their highest realization. *Money, sex,* and *pleasure* cannot satisfy our deepest urgings. When meshed with love, altruism, and sacrifice, functional actions take on energies of ultimate experiences. Hence, money earned by a parent assumes ultimate proportions when he or she labors to keep the family together. Ultimacy also exists when a husband and wife's deep love culminates in sexual intercourse.

Altruism is ultimate, whereas power is functional. Altruistic activity, like volunteering in a soup-kitchen, affords no

monetary rewards but connects us to the core of our humanity. On the other hand, *power* for power's sake is functional.
Power may become ultimate when it is exercised for the common good.

Finally, core and primary dispositions move us toward the
ultimate, which relates to the *end or purpose of life.* Our ultimate purpose is to find fulfillment, love, and happiness, not
to live in an affluent suburb, exercise power, or become rich.
The latter are *means* to an end, not ends in themselves. All
functional endeavors can help us achieve our ultimate goal.

Happy people balance ultimate and functional life dimensions. They find ultimate answers to ultimate questions and
functional answers to functional ones. If a person needs a
parent's love, material gifts are not sufficient. If a skilled computer operator is required, an employee who engages the
office staff in ultimate conversation will not do.

Receiving functional answers to ultimate questions or ultimate answers to functional questions often results in alienation, frustration, or unhappiness. Stressing the ultimate
and neglecting the functional leads to aimlessness, laziness,
and irresponsibility, whereas emphasizing the functional and
neglecting the ultimate results in meaningless ambiguity.

Modes of Human Response[6]

Core, primary, and secondary mythic meanings are closely
allied with core, community, and consideration modes of
human response.[7] The *core mode* touches our innermost
being; community involvement relates to the *community
mode;* and problem solving through rational analysis belongs
to the *consideration mode.*

Like a swirl or spiral, dynamics involved in the relationship
between these modes move from deep within a person, where
the human spirit is energized (core), to the outer limits of
human consciousness (consideration). The entire movement
flows through group response (community), as society, fam-

ily, friends, work and culture shape peoples' attitudes and values.

The *core mode* is the deepest dimension of the person, from which human energy ultimately emerges. Here primal urges move us to search for core mythic meaning. This wellspring roots life's meaning system. Spiritual energy, creative awareness, and intuitive insights as well as awe, beauty, and wonder emerge from this groundwork of creation.

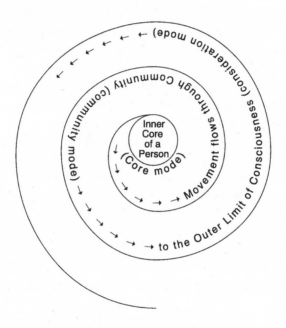

Questions flowing from the core mode cannot be programmed. This mode enables people from different cultural and religious beliefs to relate deeply with ultimate experiences or deep personal stories. The core mode moves us to search for meaning beyond functional activities such as making money or going to the store. It roots our need to find happiness, meaning, joy, and peace.

The *community mode* involves deep interactions between family members, friends, or other communities. Here we search for primary mythic meaning. The orientation of a particular community influences how its symbol systems filter the energies flowing from the core mode. This happens when a mother puts her arm around her son and forgives him or when a Native American prays for healing in the sweat-lodge ritual. Hence, cultural, historical, and personal beliefs affect the way the community mode actualizes the energies coming from the core mode.

The core mode is linked with community action. Sometimes these links are positive, leading to love, cooperation, and trust. At other times, negativity results, as jealousy, bickering, and destructive competition permeate a group. Positive links satisfy core dispositions; negative links frustrate them.

The *consideration mode* uses rational thought to plan activities, construct projects, analyze results, or rationally reflect on actions and beliefs. This mode is the proper focus of intellectual discourse, business models, faith formulae, rational analyses, and philosophical statements.

The consideration mode, a vital part of the human enterprise, cannot be dichotomized from it. Here we discover secondary mythic meaning, for by making functional work possible, it helps us achieve our goals.

──────Key Structuring Factors in Any Society──────

Just as animals respond to life events through well-determined instincts, so humans are governed by basic factors that set the tone for our attitudes and activities. This applies to entire societies, such as the United States, and to particular groups, such as a family, club, business, or church.

Two months passed before Ben spoke a word in my college class. He avoided association with me and class members. His peers regarded him as an antisocial loner. His long hair and slovenly demeanor reflected a rebellious, angry spirit. He never said much the entire semester and passed with a C grade.

I forgot about Ben until three years later, when I taught an upper-division class. A well-dressed man sat before me with a familiar name, which I failed to identify. The student smiled, cooperated, and never missed class. One day, the student remained after class. He asked, "Do you remember me? I was in your class three years ago and rarely said anything. You probably don't recognize me without my long beard and sloppy clothes. I'd like to make an appointment to see you."

When we met, Ben said, "I really got a lot out of your freshman class, even though I never showed it. That's why I signed up for this one. Before the semester began, I decided to shave and clean up. Maybe I wanted to prove something to you, or maybe to myself."

Rather puzzled, I responded, "That's great!" Ben replied, "I can't expect you to understand, until I tell you what's been going on in my life the past five years." He began, "In high school, I was a star basketball player, made national rating polls for college prospects, and had scholarship offers from top schools. In my final game, I severely injured my back. The doctors said my playing days were over. The schools withdrew their scholarship offers."

He continued, "For four years, I felt sorry for myself, rebelled and withdrew. This summer, I recalled what you said three years ago about life's meaning. When school began, I saw the need to start over, after I realized it was time to stop feeling sorry for myself and get on with life?"

Ben turned his life around, did well in his senior year, graduated, and began a successful career. His story serves as a backdrop to consider the fundamental ways that human life is structured. Until Ben was hurt, he never had any serious ups and downs. He was secure and affirmed, largely because of basketball. When this was taken away, his inner and outer worlds changed.

Ben no longer found his identity in basketball. Cheering

crowds and fan congratulations ceased. The outer world, shaping his value orientation, disappeared. Ben entered another world, that he could not accept.

An individual, society, group, family, organization, meeting, or church is structured by two basic factors, namely, the person's or group's *mythos* and *rituals*. *Mythos* refers to the fundamental orientation of a society, group, or individual. The mythos structuring Ben's life before his injury emphasized basketball. His high school world, centering on basketball, included pep rallies, dances, school assemblies, trophy rooms, and school announcements. Ben's mythos was real for him. It gave him identity, support, and a college education. Ben's injury shattered this mythos.

Rituals act out or celebrate a group's or person's mythos. Most of Ben's activities before he was hurt were structured ritualistically around basketball. He told me, "I ate, slept, and drank basketball." When his mythos collapsed, this changed.

The meaning, power, and direction of human actions happen within a certain mythos and its ritualistic interaction. While a basketball star, Ben read sports magazines, attended college games and regarded basketball as a powerful symbol. After his injury, it became a countersymbol, associated with loneliness and depression.

Ben's story illustrates the key structuring agents of any group or individual's life, namely, mythos and rituals. It also indicates that meaningful actions relate to the mythos and rituals within which they develop.

Ben's need to find meaning after basketball connected with his search for core and primary mythic meaning. In his senior year of college he let go of the past and refocused his mythos and ritual patterns into new configurations. Only then did his life make sense again. Ben's story indicates how the "within" of human dispositions was influenced by the "without" of his cultural and human experience in his pursuit of meaning.

5

A Disheveled Man: Meaning and Mythos

M y emotional response at closing the old savings account came from the lifelong relationship between my father and me. All of life is influenced by events that shape us.

Core dispositions, common to every person (the within), take different shape as they are influenced by the mythos and rituals of family, neighborhood, society, or culture (the without).

PERSON	SOCIETY
Core Dispositions	Mythos-Rituals of a given family, group, or society
(The "within")	(The "without")

This chapter considers mythos and society, dimensions of mythos, and healthy or distorted mythos.

Mythos and Society

Mythos and rituals, the two fundamental structuring agents in any group, cannot exist without each other. They are oppo-

site sides of the same coin. Every societal mythos is celebrated or lived out in ritual actions, which help clarify a
group's mythos.

*Mythos is a fundamental orientation that establishes the
groundwork for the attitudes, values, behavior, and activities
of a group or an individual.*[1]

Every business, culture, family, classroom, office, church,
and neighborhood has a different mythos. Often we clarify
aspects of a group mythos through stories. The following stories illustrate various mythical perspectives.

Business

Charles operated a successful consulting firm in a small town on the
East Coast of the United States. Occasionally Mr. James, vice-pres-
ident of a large corporation, conducted business with him. On one
occasion, Mr. James told Charles that he was impressed with his
dedication, personality, intelligence, and commitment. He said,
"Charles, expect a job offer from me that you won't be able to refuse.
I hope to become president of our corporation. When that happens,
I want you to come to Atlanta and be one of my vice-presidents."

About nice months later, Mr. James called to arrange a visit with
Charles. At the meeting, Mr. James didn't waste words. He said,
"Recently I received word of my promotion to the presidency of our
company. I am now in a position to offer you a vice-president's job,
but there is one condition. You must begin this job immediately. I
need you in Atlanta by next Monday."

Charles was flattered by the offer, yet stunned by the immediacy
of the move. He responded, "I can come to Atlanta for a few days next
week, but I have business and family responsibilities at home."

"A few days! You don't get it," said Mr. James, "I need you in
Atlanta permanently next week. You have to move in by then. After
all, I am making you vice-president of the corporation."

Charles continued, "That's impossible. Even if I finished my personal business from Atlanta, what about my wife and five children?
My family needs me."

Mr. James replied, "Your family! If that's your worry, consider
doing what I did in a similar situation fifteen years ago."

Charles inquired. "What did you do?" Mr. James replied, "It was a clear-cut decision for me. I divorced my wife, left my children, and came to Atlanta. Look what it got me. I am now president of the corporation! You could be my successor some day."

Charles found it hard to believe what he heard. He refused to go to Atlanta and never heard again from Mr. James.

Charles and Mr. James reflect different fundamental orientations toward life, family, and business. These perspectives establish the groundwork for their attitudes, values, behavior, and actions. They shape their responses, by providing lenses through which each man makes his decisions.

Charles's mythos is based on family priorities. Mr. James's mythos does not contain these values. He cared little about Charles's family, thereby revealing his shallow commitment to functional values associated with success and money.

Both men's ritualistic actions were consistent with their mythos. Charles's refusal to accept Mr. James's offer reveals a mythos that places priority on family and personal integrity. Mr. James's mythos lead him to choose business success over family solidarity.

Culture

Samantha came to the United States from an Asian country fifteen years ago and took a job with a company on the West Coast. One day, without previous notice, her manager summarily dismissed her, giving no adequate reasons for his action.

Company officials soon discovered the manager erred in letting her go. For political reasons, they refused to reinstate her. She filed a lawsuit. Concerned about a large financial settlement for her unjust firing, they offered Samantha a settlement.

She refused the money, demanding a written apology from the company, admitting they were wrong. This would restore her good name. The executives found it hard to believe she did not have another motive.

A lengthy court case ensued and it was settled only when the company agreed to give her a letter of apology.

Samantha's cultural mythos, which says that one's name

and reputation are more important than money, was different from the company's mythos. The company's mythos, centered on money, missed this completely.[2]

Classroom

Professors in two graduate classes have different attitudes toward their students. In the first class, Dr. George engages students in a mutual learning endeavor. Caring about all of them, he is particularly attentive to those having difficulties. His enthusiasm motivates students to do their best. Soon after the semester begins, they realize that his class is oriented toward student growth.

Most students find the second class, taught by Dr. Marcus, cold and impersonal. Only a few of his favorites receive attention. They hang around before and after class, get praise when answering questions and receive good grades.

If students do not belong to his select few, they initially feel they don't count. Then, figuring out what is happening, they often get mad, but know they have to keep their mouths shut to get a good grade. The basic orientation of this class is, "You don't count unless you play up to the professor and tell him how great he is."

Dr. George's mythos makes students feel important and confident of their abilities. The class environment he creates is conducive to the adult learning process. On the other hand, Dr. Marcus's mythos, giving preference to a few, alienates the rest. His superior attitude is revealed in the way he structures this class. Except for select people, the students learn very little.

Family

The Smith family—mother, father, and four children—are outgoing, support one another, and welcome others into their home. Neighbors feel part of the family. The Smiths have little money, but their love, faith, and neighborly concern reveal their mythos. The parents set the basic orientation which establishes a physical, spiritual, and emotional structure that results in this healthy family.

The Edgar family—mother, father, and one child—is different.

Both parents are on the fast track. Jim, their eight-year-old child, rarely sees his parents during the week. They take him to day care around 7:00 each morning. From there, he goes to school and back to day care until 6:00 P.M., when they pick him up again. Then they grab a bite to eat at a fast food restaurant and shop. Too tired after returning home to spend quality time with one another, they do household chores, watch television, and go to bed. Jim's grandparents, who take care of him almost every weekend, notice that Jim never smiles.

Jim's unhappiness is a reaction to his parents' mythos. The unspoken mythical perspective in Jim's parents' mythos tells him, "You are not as important as our upscale lifestyle. Time spent with you must take a back seat, so we can continue our high-pressured careers."

Core dispositions are adequately fulfilled in the mythos of the Smith family but not in that of the Edgar family. Whenever core dispositions mesh satisfactorily with family, society, or group contexts, core and primary mythic meaning can be realized.

Society

Fifty years ago, I worked in my father's store in a poor neighborhood. We welcomed black and white people as friends. They responded to this fundamental orientation of our store. They knew they could come in, be respected, get assistance and feel equal to my Dad, the white store owner.

The same wasn't true in society at large. I learned this lesson on a family vacation to Florida. Driving through the southern states, signs stating, "No Colored Welcome in this Restaurant," "Bathrooms for Whites Only," and "No Colored on this Bus," stunned me. "Why is this the case?" I thought, "Black people are welcome in our store. They are my friends." The mythos of our family store toward blacks differed from what existed in other places. Our welcome and support of blacks contrasted with the refusal of southern businesses to admit them.

As society eventually improved its attitude in racial matters, so it also changed its attitude toward women. When I graduated from high school over forty-five years ago, only a few of my female classmates went to college. The ones that did usually became teachers or nurses. During this era, most high school women married soon after graduation, had children, and worked in their homes. Today women's mythos is different, as they struggle for equal rights in all phases of society.

Different mythical perspectives exist in business offices, families, churches, neighborhoods, and society at large. The pressure to follow a prevalent group mythos exerts considerable influence on adolescents, friends, and business associates.

Mythos is such a part of peoples' lives that they rarely reflect on it. It has great power to shape our attitudes, values, and activities both positively and negatively. Functioning primarily on the level of the preconscious, mythos establishes our fundamental orientation. Its deepest dimensions cannot be adequately analyzed through abstract discourse or expressed in words. Stories or myths come closest to expressing its full meaning.[3]

Dimensions of Mythos

People develop their mythos in relation to the group mythos that shaped them by accepting some mythical elements and rejecting others. This is a complex process involving various elements relating to core, primary, and secondary mythic meaning.[4] The story of Sam, a corporate executive, illustrates some of these elements.

Sam is a man of high principles, moral integrity, and deep religious values. Several years ago, he took a job in a northwestern town as a regional director of company operations. He soon realized that some corporate transactions involved questionable ethical practices. He began to correct this situation, but knew he had to maintain company profitability. Through good management, a supportive office environment, and excellent client relations, Sam increased profits, while changing questionable practices.

Corporate officials, hearing of Sam's success, looked into his method of operation. After studying his detailed report, they realized that he changed some company practices in his region. During Sam's annual evaluation, his immediate superior met with him and his managers. To Sam's astonishment, they were fired for violating company procedures. His mode of operation threatened corporate headquarters and other regional offices. So he had to go. The questionable practices were reintroduced by Sam's successor.

Sam increased profits because he operated efficiently at the level of secondary mythic meaning. Whereas employees previously felt stifled in their work, Sam encouraged an open relationship where employees could question and improve company procedures. Within this positive environment, customer purchases increased. But Sam also threatened his employers' primary and core mythic meaning through honesty and openness, as he blended the ultimate and functional into his work. His approach challenged their questionable practices, so he was fired. They found meaning only in profit (secondary mythic meaning); primary and core meaning meant little to them.

Core, Primary, and Secondary Mythic Meaning

The search for meaning involves a reciprocal relationship between core dispositions and the outside world. The mythos, emerging from this reciprocity, sets the direction for discovering secondary, primary, and core mythic meaning.

Secondary mythic meaning deals with the functional, objective, and measurable. Many people find meaning in their work. In the above stories, Charles found it in his consulting work. So did Mr. James, who offered him a vice-president's job. Likewise, Samantha found her work meaningful, before the company fired her. Dr. George and Dr. Marcus enjoyed teaching. Functional activities are necessary for health, enjoyment, and survival. We discover meaning in them, but work for work's sake never satisfies our longing for core and primary mythic meaning.

However, if work is associated with personal responsibilities, ultimate values, or purpose, it assumes a deeper mythic meaning. Many engineers find satisfaction knowing their work enables people to live happier, healthier lives. Research scientists experience meaning, believing their medical, scientific, and technological breakthroughs will better humankind. Human labors intensify in meaning when they allow others to live more productive lives.

This becomes evident when reflecting on Bill's way of dealing with customers. He makes eyeglasses.

Bill studies each eyeglass prescription with great care. When the person's glasses are ready, Bill fits the glasses with a big smile. His demeanor says he made them as a gift to help another human see better.

Bill's office mythos creates an environment that welcomes every person who enters. This mythos goes beyond selling eyeglasses. The latter activity takes on primary mythic meaning, because Bill derives satisfaction from his caring attitude and first-class job. This pleases him and his customers.

While some functional activities associated with secondary mythic meaning bring satisfaction, others are out of focus. Rev. Troy experienced such distortion after he met Tim at a party.

After a few drinks, Tim began bragging of his business success. Then he told the minister about problems with his wife and children and asked him if he would see him sometime the next week. Rev. Troy gave the man his card, and he called him the next day for an appointment.

They met two weeks later. For the first hour, Tim described the great man he was. He owned several corporations and bragged about millions of dollars he made over the last few years. The minister wondered when he would get around to what he wanted to discuss. Eventually, Tim got to the point of his coming. He said, "I've had problems with my wife, Sara, and my three teenage children. Sara threatened to divorce me and the kids hardly talk to me."

Rev. Troy asked how much time he spent with them. Tim answered defensively, "I don't have much time for them. I travel or work late almost every night, so I can provide everything they want."

The minister asked what they wanted. Tim continued, "My three children need new cars each year to keep up with their wealthy friends. My wife constantly requires new clothes, furniture, and household appliances."

Rev. Troy asked, "Did you ever ask if they need all these things?" Tim replied, "Well, no, I just figured they want them. By showering them with such gifts, I show my love."

The minister continued, "Do you ever go to your children's school functions, ball games, or dance recitals?" "No," he replied. "That's my wife's job. I make the money."

The conversation went nowhere. Toward the end of the appointment, Tim seemed to soften, wondering if he needed to change his approach. As Tim left, he said, "Good Evening!" and stepped out the door.

Then, suddenly he returned, took out his wallet, and gave Rev. Troy a one-hundred-dollar bill. "What's that for?" he inquired. "It's yours, in payment for your time." When the minister told him he doesn't take money for talking to people, Tim's face reddened. He shouted, "Take it, take it. Don't you know this is the only thing in life that counts!"

Rev. Troy never saw Tim again. A few months later, his wife filed for a divorce and his children refused to have anything to do with him. Tim's story indicates how the inordinate desire to find meaning in secondary mythic activities associated with money blurs a person's priorities.

We discover *primary mythic meaning* as the urgings, coming from our core mythic level, are satisfied in meaningful relationships with nature, society, and other persons. This is illustrated in the story of a transient man who visited a church one Sunday morning.

Shortly after Mass began, a disheveled man entered the back of church. He stood in the second-to-last pew on the right. The man was tall and thin, with unkempt hair and a stringy beard. After a few moments, those next to him, in front of him, and behind him moved away from the stranger. By homily time, he stood alone at the end of the pew. As I looked at him, I wondered if the man had an odor, was dirty, or had been drinking. When Communion time came, I got my answer.

The man approached the altar, smiled, and put out his hand. I said, "Body of Christ," and the man answered, "Thank you." He was not drinking, his clothes were old, not dirty, but he had an odor.

The man did not return to the back of the church, but sat instead in the front pew on the right. I thought little of the man's change in location, until I stood to conclude the Mass.

At that point, the man politely asked me to sit down for a moment. He stood in the front of church, facing the congregation. He remained silent for a long time, as all eyes in church watched him. Then he spoke, "People, look at me! Look at me! I am a human being just like you. Won't you please be kind to people like me." Then he returned to his place in the front of church.

The congregation waited in anticipation until Mass was over, eager to find out the man's identity. As the people sang the final song, he quickly left by the side door.

When the liturgy was concluded, many people looked for him outside. He was gone and was heard from no more. In my more reflective moments, I sometimes wonder, "Who was he?"

This man found no meaning in the congregation's response. His need to be welcomed was met with rejection. On the level of primary mythic meaning, this church failed him.

Rejection is widespread, whenever there is insensitivity to peoples' needs. Children feel rejected when parents place greater priority on money than them. People sense it whenever bureaucracies, schools, neighborhood gatherings, or churches treat them like numbers. When core and secondary mythic meaning are not addressed in a supportive, caring atmosphere, it is hard to experience primary mythic meaning.

Samantha, the woman who demanded a letter of apology to restore her good name, operated from the level of primary mythic meaning. The Asian cultural mythos, which shaped her belief system, taught that honor and good reputation take precedence over money. Embedded within Samantha's mythos are values that enable her to keep life in focus when challenged by difficult situations.

Such values permit us to experience meaningful relationships. When we compromise them, we lose the trust of others and human communications becomes difficult.

Some people's mythos prefers drugs, sex, and monetary gain to solid moral values. Values that are antithetical to those coming from core dispositions may be vicarious substitutes for what is lacking in their lives. In this climate, when core dispositions are not realized, some form of alienation results.

The search for *core mythic meaning* includes a quest for identity, life's purpose, ultimate destiny, a reason for living, an explanation for suffering, and the desire for transcendence. It also includes acknowledgment of limits, wonder about God's existence, desire to love and be loved, and hope for fulfillment.

The degree to which we discover such meaning is influenced by how we interiorize core values. This can be seen in the cases of Charles, who refused to abandon his wife and children in order to take the job in Atlanta; of Dr. George, whose teaching deeply influenced his students; and of Sam, who was fired for honest business practices.

Since their actions flowed from a deep level of core mythic meaning, they maintained their values when faced with conflicting situations. The same cannot be said about Mr. James and Dr. Marcus. Their inability to link values coming from the core mythic level with their response to people, led to the lack of personal fulfillment.

Groups or individuals fulfill their potential when they actualize the deep movements coming from core dispositions.
Human experience, mythology, and religious traditions reveal
various ways that societies address such movements.

Human Potential

In the search for meaning, every mythos needs to include four
interwoven aspects to fulfill the deepest needs coming from
core dispositions. These needs relate to peoples' relationship
with the mystery of Being, the universe, other humans, and
one's life journey. Joseph Campbell, a sociologist, describes
them as the "metaphysical or mystical, cosmological, sociological and psychological" functions of myth.[5]

The *metaphysical function* of mythos addresses issues
coming from core dispositions.[6] They include ultimate questions such as, Where did I come from? Why am I here at all?
Where am I going? Why is there suffering? Is there a god? A
healthy mythos addresses on an intimate level such metaphysical questions, which deal with the nature of beauty,
truth, justice, being, happiness and goodness.

Earlier societies tended to give ultimate answers to such
issues, which were embedded within their mythos. At the center was their view of God. Beginning with creation stories,
their mythical perspectives suggested answers to such questions, and they incorporated these answers into their life orientation, family, social, religious, and political structures.
These mythical elements helped people discover this first
function of mythos.

This metaphysical function helps us realize ". . . what a
wonder the universe is" and helps us experience "awe before
this mystery. . . ."[7] It helps us appreciate that mystery and
wonder underlie all human experience. Functional myths
cannot adequately address this function. The most they can
offer is functional answers to ultimate questions.

A society's attitude toward the metaphysical influences its
cosmological myths.[8] The *cosmological function* of mythos

enables people to appreciate their relationship with the stars, planets, water, earth, elements, plants, and animals.

Ancient peoples experienced the cosmos as a living organism, not as inert matter. They felt a deep harmony with the universe. Peoples' view of the cosmos relates to their ontology. Judeo-Christianity believes that one God created all things from nothing. One Hindu tradition explains human origins from a great cosmogonic egg. An Inuit tribe attributes creation to the "Old Woman of the Sea." Each mythos helps its people acknowledge their place within the universe. As with the ontological function, the cosmological one establishes an ultimate bonding between us and the world. This bonding satisfies deep urges coming from core dispositions.

An impersonal society makes it difficult to discover ultimate connections with the broader world. When this is missing, it becomes easier to manipulate nature, plunder the landscape, destroy rain forests, and drive plant and animal species into extinction.

The *sociological function* of mythos addresses the human search for meaning in relation to other humans.[9] Some societies accomplish this function better than others. A healthy social mythos gives answers that satisfy deep demands of core dispositions.

The mythos of earlier civilizations permeated every aspect of life. In giving clear directions about where humans fit into the social structure, people knew what they could and could not do. They realized satisfaction on earth and a reward hereafter by following the dictates of their particular mythos.[10]

Contemporary society suggests many ways to fulfill the sociological function of mythos, including the movement toward equality between races and sexes, opportunities for better education and universal employment, and healthier ways to support senior citizens. At the same time, because our society addresses inadequately the cosmological and ontological functions, such wonderful accomplishments often lack deep roots.

The *psychological function* of mythos helps fulfill human core dispositions by suggesting a life path for us to follow, beginning at birth and lasting one's entire life.[11] In other words, it offers us a road map, or markers along life's way to steer us in the right direction.

Traditional societies incorporated this mythical function into various rites of passage. At key times—birth, adolescence, marriage, joy, suffering, old age, and death—significant rites of passage provided courage and direction, giving people confidence in what was happening and why. These rites helped them fulfill key dynamics coming from core dispositions by enabling them to act out the directives embedded in their cultural mythos.

Earlier civilizations incorporated such psychological aspects into their mythos and rituals. These pertained differently to men, women, children, workers, hunters, sailors, fishers, farmers, warriors, slaves, free persons, nobles, kings, shamans, priests, and prophets. From a psychological viewpoint, clear directives assimilated from their social myths afforded people assistance on life's journey.

Fifty years ago, society provided more road maps than today. More stable families afforded solid direction as children grew to maturity. Churches provided clear moral directions that members followed. The role of adolescence was more clearly defined. Gradually, many stable myths broke down. As this happened, society provided fewer ultimate directions that satisfied peoples' core dispositions.

Although many families, churches, schools, and other groups still provide solid directions for a meaningful life, many secular myths stress finding happiness in money and pleasure. Instead of spiritual heroes, these myths often glorify sports figures and entertainers, whose personal lives may not offer a solid blueprint for a good life.

When disillusioned by such myths, people often "go it on their own." They search for life's meaning as solitary travelers, looking for a better balance of ultimate and functional values in order to live a meaningful existence.

Mixed Mythical Elements:
Ultimate and Functional

A group's mythos is a complex mosaic operating on many levels. It shifts focus as situations, leadership, and people change. Included are a blend of ultimate and functional elements. Their relationship influences the adequacy of the mythos in meeting peoples' needs. This blend of ultimate and functional elements exists in every family. Family members strive to maintain a healthy, happy home through their love and the work required to maintain a household.

In work situations, employees have functional duties, which may include preparing reports, analyzing data, doing manual labor, or conducting meetings. At the same time, employers often encourage workers to act responsibly and enjoy their work associates.

A group's mythos can be viewed according to the degree that ultimacy or functionalism sets its basic orientation. A mythos may be strongly ultimate, strongly functional, or contain a reasonable balance of both elements.

Many ancient civilizations were *strongly ultimate*. Although people worked hard, a religious orientation permeated their social mythos. Creation myths, religious practices, and tribal loyalty reflected this ultimacy. Religious communities such as Trappist monks and cloistered nuns reflect an ultimate mythos. Their days center on prayer, solitude, and work. Even functional activities, like making cheese or farming, are directed toward the ultimate goal of salvation. The mythos of some Eastern cultures and Third World countries tends toward the ultimate. Family, honor, loyalty, and religious belief often set the tone for peoples' decisions.

Many loving, caring families in our country focus their lives around ultimate values, like justice, compassion, care, and respect. In such families, relationships take precedence over affluence, and decisions are based on the family's ultimate good, not on prestige, money, or power.

But *strongly functional* elements exist in United States'

society. Many occupations require highly specialized workers with specific abilities. Business, commerce, engineering, nursing, and most professions require functional skills. These are necessary to work efficiently in a society that is increasingly dependent on the execution of specific tasks, like computer programming, data analysis, and managing workers. In these occupations, the predominant mythos must reflect strong functional elements.

Such a heavy dose of functionalism, inherent in wide sectors of today's society, affects people's thinking and acting. It needs to be balanced with the ultimate. Otherwise, our lives can become very impersonal.

When I was a boy, most people knew the local butcher, tavern keeper, grocer, and lawyer by name. Even the area politician was accessible: he often was in the neighborhood to chat with people, and he obtained passes to certain Washington buildings for those planning to visit the nation's capital.

During these years, a neighborhood doctor was readily accessible without an appointment. Often a nurse was present in the physician's office. If people were sick, the doctor made house calls. If one had to go to the emergency room or into the hospital, there was little red tape. If people wanted to talk to their minister, they stopped in at church or waited until their spiritual leader visited their neighborhood. Rarely did parishioners have to make an appointment. Ministers were neighbors and friends, often seen at the grocery store or on the ball field. People knew and loved such ministers, for they were there when people needed them.

Today few people stop to say hello to their doctor or attorney in medical conglomerates or large law firms. Nor do they call unannounced at their church to greet the pastor or expect to see him or her in the neighborhood. There remain few local grocers, butchers, or pharmacists.

At times, government and church bureaucracies reinforce this functional mythos. So do arguments about health care reform. Members of a church congregation allowed a functional mythos to affect their reaction to three people, who entered a Sunday service wearing motorcycle helmets.

Some parishioners were shocked, wondering if an unruly gang had entered their midst. The strangers never took off their helmets. But upon closer examination, they did not look like the motorcycle type. The woman was bent over and the men seemed nervous.

As they walked up the aisle to receive Communion, a parishioner addressed them from the pew, saying "You can't receive Communion, unless you take off those helmets." The three panicked and ran out the back door.

Later, a parishioner found out that they came from a recently established home for epileptics in the neighborhood. Under doctor's orders, they kept their helmets on, lest they hurt themselves during a seizure.

Fortunately, the situation was corrected, after parish leaders learned their identity. A pastoral minister visited them and apologized, and the congregation offered them a real welcome the following Sunday.

Establishing a healthy balance between the ultimate and functional on a global, national, local, family, and individual scale is a challenge. It may require a fundamental shift in how people treat one another. Exploitative attitudes, centered on the profit motive, change slowly. Not until countries and individuals respect one another can there be a healthy blend of the ultimate and functional. To turn this around, we need to find ways to base our lives on healthy, balanced values.

Cultural Mythos:
Open and Closed Societies

Many variations exist in the mythical perspectives of Canadians, Afro-Americans, Mexicans, Vietnamese, Australians, Filipinos, Chinese, and other peoples. Each group's underlying cultural mythos establishes parameters for different life orientations, as it refracts the common core dispositions within a specific social context.

We search for core, primary, and secondary mythic meaning within our cultures. This applies especially to primary mythic meaning, which involves relationships with nature, individuals, groups, relationships that are filtered through our cultural mythos.

A society's openness influences its mythos. Communist Russia, before it collapsed, controlled its citizens through a narrowly defined, fear-based mythos that structured peoples' thoughts and actions in a relatively closed society. When communism collapsed, this changed. Today, Russia and former Soviet bloc countries deal with the massive changes involved whenever a relatively closed society moves to a more open one.

Every family, business, and church differs in its degree of openness. This affects mythical perspectives within the group and influences peoples' attitudes toward responsibility, freedom, work, family, and church. A relatively closed religious society, like the Amish culture, places strong obligations on members to conform to dress codes and to follow traditional norms that prohibit using electricity at home, driving cars, or owning a telephone. Amish people exercise their freedom, creativity, and responsibility within their closely knit mythos. But there is adaptation within the Amish mythos. Some Amish communities allow members to drive in non–Amish-owned vehicles or to use electric tools in carpentry professions. They engage non-Amish neighbors to take telephone calls for them, which they return on public telephones. Other Amish people may not accept all of these practices. In any society that has a common mythos, variations exist.

The shift from a relatively closed mythos to a more open one can be seen in the Roman Catholic Church. Before Vatican II (1960–1964), this church manifested many characteristics of a closed society. Church authorities exercised strong influence on their members. Most Catholics accepted all church teachings, attended Sunday Mass, abstained from eating meat on Fridays, and followed rules of fast and abstinence during Lent. For Catholics, church law reflected God's will.

Today's Catholic Church is different. It is a more open society, struggling to clarify the Catholic mythos in light of the changes brought about by Vatican II, while remaining faithful to its basic beliefs and practices. Such changes brought it into dialogue with Episcopalian, Lutheran, Methodist, and other congregations interested in pursuing open dialogue among Christians.

No single description captures satisfactorily the dynamics operative in changing mythical patterns. Although leaders play a prominent role in shaping the climate for a developing mythos, each group possesses a life of its own, which cannot be fully controlled. Even in a closed society, strong mythical forces may be at cross-purposes, with leaders and members differing as to particular beliefs and ways of acting.

Mythos: Healthy or Distorted

Our mythos strongly affects our way of acting. A social worker, believing that her work alleviates someone's poverty, may spend hours without pay working with the poor. A business person, motivated by a desire for affluence, may work long hours to make money. Although every mythos is real for those subscribing to it, the question remains, How healthy or distorted is this mythos?

Out of Kilter with Its Intended Purpose

A mythos easily can become distorted. For example, a distorted mythical perspective is found in a factory where managers are more interested in promotions than in workers' safety. This mythos treats people as things to be used and then discarded. One worker referred to this kind of factory as a "a meat market."

Distortions exist in churches where cliques form, politics dominate, and new parishioners feel like intruders. They are found in religious organizations, where money managers, multiple committees, and executive staffs take priority over the group's religious mission.

One such church received pressure from its finance committee to keep the organizational structure intact but to dismiss most of its pastoral ministers. These monetary advisors never realized that the distorted organizational structure was the real problem.

Churches need organizations, meetings, and committees, but they cannot be structured according to a purely functional mythos. Whenever a church's actions are out of kilter with its intended purpose, its mythos is distorted.

Deviates From the Common Good

A healthy mythos sets the climate within which core dispositions move us to behave according to the dictates of common sense. Such a mythos is found in healthy families. A healthy family fosters mutual support. Honesty, respect, and forgiveness allow members to enjoy positive relationships, even in the midst of disappointments, conflicts, and pressures.

A distorted family mythos deviates from the common good of its members.[12] Such a mythos may tolerate abusive behavior, thereby forming a protective web of denial around the person involved. This behavior is difficult to change and sometimes requires outside assistance. Allowing it to continue fails to help the abusive person and injures the family.

Modern advertising is filled with distorted myths: one promises that using a particular product brings happiness; another glamorizes sex; still another canonizes material gain. Such myths distort reality and hurt the common good by inducing skepticism, distrust, and injustice.

While every civilization takes pride in its achievements, undue commitment to country can lead to neglecting the common good of other nations. This happens when one country exploits another to satisfy its own desires. The distorted mythos of Hitler's Nazi Germany was real for those advocating this political system. It moved its adherents to violate basic moral tenets and to commit atrocious crimes.

No mythos is completely healthy. Nonetheless, a relatively healthy one sets the climate within which our core dispositions can move us to develop acceptable modes of action.

The third millennium offers a great opportunity to devise new ways to satisfy ultimate needs in a functional world. This requires living ultimately in a society that offers few directions for accomplishing this goal. It means finding a blueprint that balances functional and ultimate needs. Such a balance often calls for a reorientation of our mythical perspectives. It cannot happen randomly, as we move pragmatically from one event to the next. For individuals, this means finding better ways to balance the ultimate and functional. This may require refocusing our personal priorities by concentrating more on people and less on money. It might mean seeking support from like-minded persons. For families, it may involve putting family solidarity above economic gain, while taking more time with one another in activities like celebrating family days or limiting Sunday activities to family, church, and relaxation. It may even require eliminating certain activities that keep parents and children from spending time together. For business and government, a good balance between the ultimate and the functional leads to a greater respect for people. Business and civic leaders can set the tone in creating a society conducive to healthy, productive lives.

6

A Thanksgiving Gift: Stories, Myths, and Meaning

The picture on the cover of the old Glenway savings book triggered strong emotions. The dynamics involved in this response sprang from my mythos, which developed from a lifetime of experiences with my father.

This mythos involved a complex pattern of personal dealings, social relationships, family happenings, work events, leisure activities, school, and church functions. Such occurrences wove an intricate web of rituals, memories, stories, values, and beliefs. Because of who I am and who my father was our mythos was unique. This mythos is reflected in various aspects of Dad's and my story. This chapter considers the relationship between mythos, myth, and story by reflecting on meaning and stories, meaning and myths, and modes of mythic meaning.

Meaning and Stories

Experiences of joy, suffering, celebration, and death provide insights into the human search for meaning. They underpin every person's story, forming pillars upon which emotional and spiritual life develops. Such experiences establish the foundation for stories and myths.

Certain events retain special importance in every person's life. Often they occur in ordinary circumstances, at times we least expect. One such event happened on Thanksgiving, when I was five years old. All day long, our family looked forward to eating the wonderful Thanksgiving meal that Mom was preparing. Shortly before we were to sit down at table, the front doorbell rang. My four-year-old sister, Mary Ann, and I ran to answer it. A boy about eleven and a girl about ten stood there. The girl held a baby, covered with a shawl. The boy said, "We are poor and have no money for food this Thanksgiving. Will you give us money, so we can buy food?" Mary Ann and I called our mother. After listening to their request, Mom answered, "We don't have much money, but we would like you to share what we have. We invite you to sit at our table and eat Thanksgiving dinner with us." The children seemed surprised, and the boy answered that they could not stay. Mom replied, "Then let us prepare three meals for you to take along with you." The children said, "Okay."

While the children waited in the hall, Mom, Mary Ann, and I went into the kitchen, prepared three meals, and put them in separate bags, one for each child. I felt very good, as we cut the turkey and arranged it on two plates for the older children. We also gave them dressing, cranberries, potatoes, beans, a piece of cake, and soda pop. Mom prepared a bottle of milk for the baby. Mary Ann and I were joyful when we gave the food to the children. They took it and left.

Since it was a beautiful day, my sister and I went onto the front porch to watch the children leave. They went down the steps and walked up the street toward the intersection. When they arrived there, the girl suddenly threw the baby to the boy. We screamed, "They are hurting the baby, they are hurting the baby!" Hurrying inside, we told Mom and Dad.

All of us returned immediately to the porch. As we got there, the girl, now holding the baby, tucked it under her arm. As she did, the boy, who carried the food, laughed in the funniest way. Then he took the Thanksgiving meals that we had lovingly prepared and threw them down the sewer. They continued laughing as they disappeared around the corner.

My sister and I sobbed, blurting out, "They hurt the baby

and threw away our food." As our emotions overcame us, Mom and Dad embraced us, while Mom said, "Bob and Mary Ann, it's okay. We are going to have a wonderful Thanksgiving." We answered, "But they hurt the baby and threw away our food."

Mom said, "The children tricked us. That was not a baby; it was a doll. They didn't want food, they only wanted money. Nevertheless, you are going to learn an important lesson today." Quieting down, we asked about the lesson. Then Mom spoke words that indelibly impressed themselves on me. What she told us, I've never forgotten. She said, "We gave the children a wonderful gift today, because we shared a big part of our Thanksgiving meal with them. That was our great gift. The fact that the children refused our gift doesn't mean our gift was not wonderful. The important thing is that we gave with a good heart."

Mom continued, "That's what God did a long time ago, when God gave us the greatest gift of all time—God's only son, Jesus. Just as the children rejected our gift this morning, some people rejected Jesus and continue to reject him through lies, deceit, and hurting one another. But God's gift of Jesus is still the greatest gift we can receive. Let's remember God's gift and our gifts today, as we go inside and have a wonderful Thanksgiving meal."

I learned more about gift giving from Mom's simple words on that Thanksgiving day than from all the books I have read on gratitude and thanksgiving. Her words remain etched into my soul. This story has been told and retold in our family. Its lesson provides a hinge, influencing our family's mythical perspectives.

Such stories have deep meaning, because they touch something real. In this way, they take us beyond the functional to an ultimate dimension.[1] To better appreciate "story," it helps to remember that every deep story touches a core level of human meaning.

Stories that profoundly affect us involve elements of *core* and *primary mythic meaning.* Our Thanksgiving story is one such story. This story developed as it was retold over the years in our family. Its core dimensions remained the same, even though details of what actually happened were recast according to different memories of family members.

The core dimensions of the Thanksgiving story included being grateful, sharing what we have with needy people, learning the meaning of a gift, discovering the pain of deceit, appreciating parental wisdom, celebrating life in ambiguous times, giving thanks, seeing the significance of God and Jesus, and developing family bonds. The story had different meanings for various family members and others beyond our family, for it touched their search for meaning on different levels. As we told the Thanksgiving story to people beyond our family, it affected individuals of different ages, races, and ethnic backgrounds.

Certain elements of every story depend on *local customs and beliefs*. An understanding of local coloring helps put a story's core and primary mythic meaning into better focus. Appreciating such elements requires knowledge of a particular culture or family tradition. For example, appreciating this Thanksgiving story presumes knowledge of the origin of Thanksgiving Day, the reason turkey is associated with this celebration, how sewers work on streetcorners, and basic belief in God and Jesus. Without this knowledge, the story's full meaning is not evident.

A story's impact doesn't depend on an exact retelling of the details as they first happened. Its core and primary mythic meanings are real no matter how exact each detail might be, as long as the story reflects the original mythos. Literal details support a story's meaning, but do not change its real message.

Hence, this story's deepest meaning would not be affected if four rather than three children had actually come to the door, if both Mom and Dad had gone onto the front porch with us, or if it recounted exactly what Mom said to Mary Ann and me when she realized the children's trickery. Such literal details often have little to do with the story's basic meaning.

As the Thanksgiving story passed *orally* through our family, it developed certain variations. The same thing happens in other families as they retell their stories to children and grandchildren, thereby passing on personal, religious, and cultural values. Several renditions of a family story may exist, indicating how different interpretations are given to a basic story, depending on the group or individual telling it.

Cultures that depend on oral communication to convey fundamental dimensions of their mythos retell their stories orally from generation to generation. In this way, core realities conveyed by the stories influence succeeding generations. This happened in every part of the globe, as early people depended on oral communication to pass on their basic beliefs to succeeding generations.

Our family also conveyed the Thanksgiving story in *writing* through letters, articles, and books. In its more formalized written versions, this Thanksgiving story is more accessible to people outside of our family.

Early civilizations told their stories around campfires, in family settings, or at religious services, before they were written down. Thanks to writing, many such stories are preserved, even though the civilizations have ceased.

Finally, the Thanksgiving story has been communicated through *technology,* as taped versions transmit its message to wider audiences. From the stuff of such stories, modern technology blesses millions of people through movies, television episodes, and videos.

——— Stories and Myths: A Universal Appeal ———

Myths originate in the human story. Through them, a communal mythos or particular aspects of it are expressed. In telling the Thanksgiving story over and over, it became a family myth. It taught us about ourselves and how to get along with others.

A community's myth expresses deep aspects of its mythos,

which reflects basic beliefs that go beyond a particular family or group. Early peoples placed great significance on such myths, especially their creation myths, that describe human origins as coming from a god, living in a realm beyond this earth. Often such myths describe a superior being creating humans from specific parts of this present world.

Ancient and modern myths encapsulate basic beliefs of the communities that developed them. Joseph Campbell says, "myths are metaphorical of spiritual potentiality in the human being, and the same powers that animate our life animate the life of the world."[2]

Every myth can have perennial appeal, because myths spring from the realm of core and primary mythic meaning. The Sumerian creation myth, *Enuma Elish,* addresses peoples' search for origins, relationships with higher powers, and their place in the universe.[3] The Ojibway myth of *Nanabush* treats the proper human response when facing life's trials and tribulations. The Greek myth of *Oedipus* addresses dimensions of a boy's sexuality in relation to his mother.

Contemporary music, television, and movies often owe their appeal to an ability to touch core and primary mythic meaning, even though such modern myths may send out inadequate messages.

The Meaning of "Myth"

Put simply, a "myth" is the way a community's mythos is expressed. Often this happens through telling the "story." In earlier times, family and tribal storytellers used stories to pass on fundamental community beliefs.

Today such communal beliefs are conveyed through speech, writing, and technology. Myth does not use a single mode of human discourse to pass on key elements of a society's mythos.

Myth is an intuitive manifestation of a community attitude about life's meaning, expressed in some concrete way and implicitly symbolizing deep-seated facets of human existence.

A myth is an *intuitive manifestation of a community's attitude about life's meaning.* Like mythos, it operates on a level deeper than reason. Although using logical powers, the ability to create myths springs from the human potential to intuit deeper aspects of reality than are apparent to reason.

The Genesis creation myth considers the struggle between good and evil in the temptation story. This story of the fall of Adam and Eve addresses the existence of evil in the world (Genesis 2:5–3:24). The myth's answer to the question Why evil? is linked with Adam and Eve's sin of disobedience. The myth implies that whenever sin occurs, evil and alienation result. This explanation of evil's origin comes from intuitive insights, inspired by the community's belief in Yahweh-God's revelation.

In today's world, a soap opera can be seen as a modern myth about what is supposed to make people happy. Unlike the Adam-and-Eve myth, such secular myths often suggest life patterns that are contrary to those dictated by God in the Genesis myth. In other words, modern myths often glorify what the Genesis myth condemns—lies, deceit, immorality, injustice, and greed. Such myths are intuitive manifestations of a society's mythos, even though their message represents distorted, functional answers to ultimate concerns.

Expressed in a concrete way. A myth uses concrete language to express its message. The Adam-and-Eve myth takes place in a garden. Concrete aspects of the story include a tree, a serpent, clothes, and swords. The latter details were well known to those for whom the story was intended.

In contemporary myths, situations known to modern readers also couch the myth. These may include professions, such as doctors, lawyers, nurses, and business executives, as well as functional devices, like computers, telephones, and fax machines.

Implicitly symbolizing deep-seated facets of human existence. The Adam-and-Eve myth reflects the universal search for fulfillment. The "garden" represents peoples' desire for paradise and full human happiness. The myth also indicates the reality of human alienation and loneliness, reflected in Adam and Eve's being cast from the garden. The story symbolizes the deep human desire for happiness and the need to address earthly finitude.

Modern soap operas search for similar fulfillment, acknowledge alienation, and offer solutions to the human plight. Unlike the Genesis myth, their solutions frequently rest on pleasure, casual sex, money, power, and instant gratification.

Kinds of Myth

A subtle difference exists between mythos and myth. *Mythos* refers to a fundamental orientation that establishes the groundwork for a group's overall attitudes, values, and responses. *Myth* indicates the way the mythos is expressed. Various dimensions of a group's mythos can be expressed in different ways.

Although some myths are more clearly articulated than others, most mythic themes, inherent in the way a group operates, are not spelled out in a definite way. Take, for instance, the different mythical patterns existing in every family. These include subtle ways in which family members convey values, attitudes, and life orientation. Such patterns manifest themselves in how family members communicate with each other. They include complex ritual patterns that dictate acceptable rules of conduct, value orientations, church affiliation, and ways of reacting to political causes or ethnic groups. They also involve expectations for eating together, family gatherings, or curfew time for teenage children.

An *implicit* myth implies key elements of the community's mythos, but not in a clearly defined way. Often such myths hint at but never articulate the deepest perspectives of a group's or individual's mythos. Many implicit myths underlie mythical patterns that group members presume in order to communicate with each other.

As our family matured, we learned definite values and developed specific modes of response as members of the Hater family. The Thanksgiving story illustrates some of these values. Even today it is not easy to clearly identify our family's implicit myths, and yet they dictated key aspects of our lives, often surfacing when we tell our stories.

Many implicit myths are associated with a family's or group's story. Their implicit content is not focused into an explicit myth, but usually assumes a clearer focus over time. The Thanksgiving story comes close to being an explicit family myth. An explicit myth clarifies what is indirectly contained in the implicit myth. The John Kennedy assassination story, told over two generations, is becoming an explicit myth, which captures elements contained in the implicit United States myth of his time.

Explicit and implicit myths are fluid categories used to indicate the degree to which a myth articulates its central themes. The temptation account in the Adam-and-Eve myth represents a clearly developed, explicit myth.[4] A modern television commercial, on the other hand, represents aspects of the implicit myth of success, pleasure, and money.

In changing times, as basic dimensions of a culture's mythos shift focus, myths are not formulated into consistent, regular patterns. This is evident in the struggle to inculturate various ethnic groups into United States society, illustrated by the civil rights movement.

Since the abolition of slavery, this country has walked in uneven steps along the road to equal rights for blacks. Their freedom was acknowledged legally but not actually practiced in many places. The 1960s brought out key elements of the black race's struggle for equality, inspired by Martin Luther King Jr.'s leadership to win voter registration, equal employment, education, employment, and housing.

This struggle continues today, as implicit mythical elements take more explicit form in civil rights legislation, business practices, and social environments. Something similar is happening in women's efforts to gain full equality with men and in the attempts of other ethnic groups to become accepted members of United States society.

After a community develops consistent patterns of belief and action, the relational patterns flowing from them may remain implicit. Such is the case in the Adam-and-Eve myth. The story hints at elements that are clarified more fully in other Hebrew community myths. They include male and female roles and the relationship between humans and God.

The communications media, especially television, movies, internet, radio, and videos, articulate implicit mythical messages that millions of people see and hear every day. This is a mixed bag. On one hand, some of its messages convey religious and moral values. Other messages glorify injustice, sex, violence, greed, power, and prestige. The latter values would make many people uneasy if they had to acknowledge them explicitly in a public forum. They would hesitate to say, "What the media portrays is my explicit myth; I live by such values."

In the latter case, such implicit elements do not give a clear picture of many peoples' mythos, even though they portray an implicit myth to be emulated and celebrated. Such subtle programming uses deep communication dynamics to distort human values, especially among the young.

An *explicit* myth brings to focused awareness significant elements of a community's implicit mythos. This is why certain stories, like the Adam-and-Eve myth, are key vehicles for developing a group's values, which are passed on to others.

The Hebrew people communicated essential parts of their mythos around campfires, told them in family gatherings, repeated them in worship services, and formulated them into laws about human dependence on God and human responsibility for one's actions. In this way, they developed explicit myths, like the Adam-and-Eve story. Various parts of the myth focus on their beliefs. The story begins with Adam and Eve's creation. At first, they are happy and content, but the serpent promises they shall be like God. Their sin leads to recognition of their nakedness and expulsion from the garden.

This story explicitly relates evil in the world to their disobedience. In this explicit myth, implicit mythical perspectives existing in the community that formulated the myth are developed as the story unfolds. Something similar happens in all great religious myths and in the myths of every country, tribe, city, family, and group, which *explicitly* focus the *implicit* myths contained in the community's mythos.

United States citizens often tell such stories on days like Labor Day, Thanksgiving, Martin Luther King's holiday, Washington's birthday, and Memorial Day. Families recount their own stories on Christmas, Easter, anniversaries, birthdays, and graduations. Such explicit myths reflect a community's implicit mythos.

Like mythos, implicit and explicit myths can be ultimate or functional. Most myths contain a mixture of these elements, although certain myths are more ultimate than others. For instance, business myths tend to be functional, whereas religious myths are more ultimate.

Ultimate myths address questions coming from human core dispositions in ways that encourage people to focus their search for meaning on an ultimate level. The Adam-and-Eve story is such a myth. It addresses fundamental human issues in ways that transcend ordinary experience. In this way it helps people deal with evil in the world.[5]

Many family myths are ultimate. They help members develop respect, trust, and goodness in their attitudes, communications, and life-styles. Many functional myths, learned in families, address aspects of life that are necessary for survival and growth. They teach children why they need to eat properly, brush their teeth, work, exercise, and take care of their clothes and toys. From them children learn that Dad and Mom may have to leave home to earn money to support the family. Such myths, explicitly or implicitly developed, form the backdrop for learning functional responsibilities.

Similar mythical patterns continue in adult life. Every

business, work situation, or secular organization operates from a variety of myths. Normally, these myths describe the company's goals and objectives.

A business organization may motivate sales representatives by telling the company's story, which describes its success in terms of efficiency, personal client contacts, high quality sales meetings, and pride in its products. This was illustrated years ago at a board of directors' meeting of a successful insurance company.

The CEO gave a positive portrayal of the company's success. He honored members of the sales force that belonged to the "Million Dollar Round Table," a group of especially successful sales persons. He stressed that the "client comes first" and said, "If we maintain this philosophy, customers will flock to us."

This meeting reflected a well-balanced company, geared to a functional myth of making money, but couched in an ultimate mythos that cared about people.

Such a myth is focused on functional, objective, scientific, or monetary goals but also includes ultimate elements such as compassion, care, understanding, justice, and truth. The need for this kind of orientation is illustrated negatively in the following story.

Several years ago, Mary, a college graduate, took her first job with a large computer company. The company's myth, described in recruitment literature, indicated an efficiently run organization with a profitable bottom line. Company executives repeatedly stressed company concern for employees and clients.

Soon after Mary began work, she discovered the company's real mythos was different from the one conveyed to her. Employees often were used, then discarded, because of company greed for more and more profit.

After a few months, Mary had had enough. She resigned and found new employment in a more human firm. Not all employees were so lucky. Eventually, company greed and disregard for people caused it to self-destruct.

Some functional myths that advertise a company's product

promise functional answers to questions that only ultimate myths can address. Such functional myths advocate secular solutions—money, power, prestige—to the deep quest for happiness. These myths are common in a secular society and are found in novels, movies, television programs, and advertising. They take center stage in contemporary life, operate within a secular perspective, and fail to fulfill deep yearnings of the human heart.

A group's mythos develops over time. It contains interwoven strands of values, directions, and modes of response. As the mythos shifts focus, its expressions also change. Often such expressions are implicit myths, depicted on television programs, advertising, music, and public airwaves. They take form through legislation, public discussions, and various modes of communication. Some implicit myths may become explicit. In this web of implicit and explicit myths various modes of mythic meaning take shape.

Myth and Modes of Mythic Meaning

One myth often reiterated in advertising, movies, music, and television programs says, "Money brings happiness." What this myth promises concerning a happy life often is not consistent with real life experiences. Many people discover that material possessions fail to bring them happiness. While possessing "things" they feel hollow inside, not knowing where they are going, what road map to follow, or what values to espouse. This money-brings-happiness myth needs to be refocused within the deeper context of the modes of mythic meaning.

United States Society

Each society addresses core, primary, and secondary modes of mythic meaning in different ways. A society's health depends on the balance between these modes.

To ensure such balance, our ancestors endured painful struggles to free us from tyranny, oppression, and allegiance to foreign governments. The Constitution guarantees inalienable rights for free people and balances individual and communal rights. The United States core myth centers on freedom and equality. In its earliest forms, this myth linked basic rights with spiritual values and a transcendent God.

Over the past hundred years, legislation and public policy have shifted this core myth, illustrated in Supreme Court decisions prohibiting prayer in public schools. Many religious values that once set the tone for peoples' freedom, rights, and responsibilities have been minimized.

This watering down of spiritual values has brought about a leveling of moral values. The result is seen in the aimless pragmatism that is evident in many myths glorified on television, legislated in court systems, and implied in education. Today's pragmatic core myth of happiness rests on secular, not transcendent, values. The resulting indifference, anger, violence, and disrespect reflect a mythos that has moved afield from the basic beliefs that first energized this country.

The original myth has faded, losing the explicit motivating power it possessed at this country's inception. Although this core myth is still implicit, today's myth has moved away from basic dynamisms that established it.[6] When an original core myth is blurred, finding meaning on primary and secondary mythic levels takes a different focus.

Originally, the United States core myth bound people together under God. It set the tone for them to discover *primary mythic meaning* in their relationships with each other. Here, they actualized the deep energies coming from core dispositions in flesh-and-blood experiences.

Gradually this myth changed. It became increasingly difficult to see ultimate relationships as normative in a culture that opted for pragmatism, relativism, materialism, and individualism as its core myth. Today a secular myth underpins the values that dominate the airwaves, television programs, businesses, politics, and schools. It affects family values and peoples' attitudes. This myth often manifests itself in children's conduct.

In earlier generations, families afforded clear messages to children. Even though young people modified family teachings as they matured, their developing personalities were established on a firm foundation. Today many families provide no relational stability. They are fragmented through divorce, separation, absentee parents, multiple-family configurations, and conflictual home situations.

In this milieu, children have no certain road map to follow. Many respond by imitating their adult role models. They pick up parental signals and learn from thousands of hours of television, viewed during their formative years. As they mature, their lives often lack direction and their attitudes become more pragmatic. In this process, society's implicit and explicit myths affect succeeding generations.

Subtle functional messages, divorced from ultimate core meaning, disrupt the search for primary mythic meaning. Consumerism distorts basic human needs, while moral relativism makes people distrustful of neighbors and government. Society's impersonalism leads to a cry for personal fulfillment, a need seldom acknowledged by the secular agenda.

A secular myth gives little recognition to core and primary mythic values. Besides disassociating the primary mythic quest from core mythic meaning, canonization of the functional makes it harder to relate on a human level. There is little time to relax, laugh, cry, and enjoy friends. People operate on a schedule that is more like a computer printout than a human life agenda. Many spouses see each other on the run. When together, often they are too tired too communicate on a deep level. No wonder they mesmerize themselves in front of television sets or spend their free time at fast food restaurants or shopping! Those who canonize the functional have one choice—find meaning on the secondary mythic level or don't find it at all.

Secondary mythic meaning, associated with functional

aspects of life, is necessary for human fulfillment. We need to feel productive, which is often associated with our work. This came home to me during a prolonged sickness.

After an automobile accident, I lost much of my strength. As days passed into months, my confidence waned and I felt useless. My teaching career, once so important, seemed a long way off. Not knowing if I would regain my strength, I went down and down. Only after my health improved and my halting efforts to get back on my feet proved successful did I regain my self-confidence. This difficult time taught me how important work is to help one fulfill one's personal meaning.

During my sickness, I found strength in my faith (core mythic meaning), family, and friends (primary mythic meaning). I wondered what it would be like without them. Life was disoriented enough, because I could not work (secondary mythic meaning). My experiences taught me how lack of work can affect people who remain unemployed for long periods of time.

United States people have unique opportunities to succeed in their work. There are many possibilities for people to contribute to humankind by using their gifts in the many occupations open to them. But when societal myths reflecting core and primary mythic meaning are out of balance, secondary mythic meaning assumes the burden of ensuring a happy life. Unfortunately many negative results flow from the priority our society gives to work and financial success. Often functional achievements are the ultimate norms for success and one's occupation assumes a higher priority than a spouse or family. When a people's myths canonize secondary mythic meaning, they need to be refocused or it may not be long before the society self-destructs.[7]

Churches

In an impersonal and individualistic world, people hunger for meaningful relationships, consistent values, and credible beliefs. Finding little meaning in their work or unable to develop relational support in broken, overburdened families, they look for deeper meaning wherever they can find it. In this effort, many people turn to churches.

Religious congregations have an opportunity to address peoples' ultimate needs. Many churches do this, as they teach moral values, celebrate religious meaningful rituals, and serve the poor. To accomplish their mission, church congregations are challenged to keep their spiritual message in the forefront, as they organize, manage, and conduct their religious business. Otherwise, the secular values that permeate daily life will influence them negatively.

Churches often use models similar to those in business to organize finances, manage employees, and strategize future plans. When a business myth sets the tone to organize a church, there are bound to be mixed results. If churches do not regularly evaluate parish activities in light of their mission, they can risk becoming just another bureaucracy with multiple offices, budgets, and policies. Lest this happen, it helps to look at churches in relation to core, primary, and secondary mythic meaning.

The *Christian core myth* believes that Jesus saves people from sin, alienation, and oppression. He taught a clear, certain message, centered on love of God and neighbor. His teaching demanded just treatment for all people. To testify to his mission, he gave his life and was raised up by his Father. He continues to live among Christians through the power of the Spirit, thus enabling them to minister in his name.

Christians believe that their deepest meaning is found in union with God through Jesus Christ. If they live in his Spirit, they can overcome sin, oppression, suffering, and death. Through Jesus' presence, the church becomes Christ's body, a community of disciples commissioned to live, proclaim, and celebrate his message of salvation through words and actions.

Jesus' life and teaching are the norm for every Christian community. Christian churches are called to welcome saints and sinners into God's kingdom, which has begun already on earth. Such congregations reject sin and its consequences as destructive of the earth and humanity. They consider it an insult to turn away from the God who never ceases to love them.

Many Christian churches pride themselves on being welcoming, faith communities. Here, people find *primary mythic meaning.* In our mobile society, welcoming churches afford a stability to individuals who are often far removed from the family and neighborhood of their origins.

For this to happen, churches need to acknowledge the multiple generations and races present in their congregations. The millennial generation, X generation, baby boomers, and older people have different needs, as do various ethnic groups that populate today's neighborhoods.

All these people need a welcoming community. If they fail to find hospitality that goes beyond saying hello as they go out of Sunday services, their needs often go unfulfilled. People need to feel part of something, not to be more isolated. Being a community member brings pride and confidence. Churches that challenge secular values by providing a definite plan for following Jesus are richly rewarded. Coming to know Jesus and studying his message offer a strong glue that binds together Christian churches and gives members guidelines for a good, moral life.

Seen from the viewpoint of the Christian core myth, churches sometimes fall short. Many people leave such communities, because they fail to find the living witnesses of Jesus' core myth. They may not feel welcome or can't reconcile Jesus' message with church structures, politics, and policies. Many wonder how Jesus' command to minister to poor, broken people relates to rigorous church laws or extravagant modes of action.

This happened in a church where a troubled woman, desperate for someone to talk to, rang the office bell. A parish minister came to the door, saw her plight, but refused to see her that day. The minister said, "Come back in a few days, since I am in a meeting now and cannot be disturbed."

The woman left and almost despaired. Eventually, through the kindness of a neighbor and a wise counselor, she got back on her feet again, but she never returned to this church.

Many churches assist people with their physical needs. Such help, associated with *secondary mythic meaning,* ranges from finding housing for people to assisting them in filling out medical or governmental forms.

Functional needs often relate to deeper levels of core and primary mythic meaning. When a poor family receives money from a church, this action goes beyond material sustenance, for it touches an ultimate need. This is illustrated in the following story.

A church-affiliated hospital took in a destitute man, gave him food, bandaged his wounds, and nursed him back to health. When leaving, he asked for his bill. The church told him to pray for their work. He promised some day to pay them back.

Years later, the hospital received the deed to a huge tract of property, given to them by the once-destitute man, who was now very wealthy. Out of gratitude for the staff's kindness in nursing him back to health, he donated this land for a hospital. Today, a large hospital stands on this site.

Providing services that afford secondary mythic meaning gives Christian churches the opportunity to link such ministries to Jesus' message. When this happens, church ministry is motivated by a spirit that is at the heart of Jesus' life and teaching.

7

Forty-seven Acres: Meaning and Mythic Change

The old savings book symbolized what happened when my mythos changed during my dad's last year of life. It also occasioned recollections of another powerful event that took the life of another father.

Colin was seven when it happened. Before then he lived happily with his mother, father, and sister in a middle-class neighborhood. A visit from his mother and a church minister while he was at the babysitter's house changed him forever.

It was about two o'clock when he saw his mother and another woman come up the steps of the apartment house where he was staying. Slowly they walked down the long corridor toward him and the babysitter. Sensing something was wrong, he ran to them and blurted out, "Mommy, something terrible has happened. I can feel it. Tell me."

The woman minister ushered him and his mom into the living room. His mother began, "Colin, you know how much Dad and I love you." "Sure, Mommy, but tell me what's wrong," he replied.

His mom broke down, sobbed, and put her arms around Colin, saying, "Your daddy accidentally shot himself while cleaning his gun. He died before the ambulance arrived." The child cried profusely. After a few moments he asked two questions, Why? and Where is he?

As this drama lived itself out on the couch, the babysitter sat in the same room holding Colin's baby sister and continued to watch a soap opera about murder and infidelity. Her insensitivity distracted

Colin, his mother, and the minister during their profound moments of grief.

In the ensuing months, the minister took a special interest in Colin and his family. With her help and that of friends, family, work associates, and church people, they survived, but were never the same as before.

This story illustrates what happens when a mythos changes *dramatically.* The fundamental attitude that grounded the attitudes, behavior, and responses of Colin's family shifted, because the father's death tore asunder their mythos.

Some mythical changes happen *gradually.* This occurs as family members mature and children leave home. It also happens in business, when changing corporate practices affect a company's operational style. As such shifts take place, fundamental changes happen in individuals and groups.

This chapter considers mythical development and change, adaptation to mythical change, dimensions of mythical change, and responses to mythic change.

──────── Mythical Development and Change ────────

Before Colin's father died, the family mythos set the tone for family attitudes, behavior, and actions. In this close-knit family, where the father worked full-time in business and the mother worked part-time in the home and part-time in a laundry, family members had many opportunities to spend time together.

During such times, the family developed regular patterns of prayer, play, and work. Colin waited daily for his father to come home from work. He obeyed clear-cut rules for visiting his neighbors and friends. Sunday was a special family day, and the family took a yearly vacation. The family mythos set the tone for their lifestyle.

This way of acting became the underlying fiber of their lives, and significant deviations from it caused unrest. Their usual responses came from a prereflective set of assumptions developed over the years. These assumptions were such a part of their lives that family members hardly examined them until the father's death. When this happened, their prereflective assumptions came to conscious awareness, as family members remembered the past, agonized over the present, and wondered about the future.

Some psychologists call this prereflective dimension of largely unarticulated attitudes and beliefs a group's "collective unconscious."[1] This sets the pattern for group and individual responses. It helps explain the influence of peer pressure, because every group places certain expectations on its members. We call this dimension of human response a group's or individual's "presumed dispositions."

Presumed dispositions are the prereflective web of attitudes, beliefs, and response modes, flowing from a group's mythos, which underlie fundamental ways in which a group or individuals within the group approach issues, plan action strategies, and respond ritualistically to life situations.

Presumed dispositions are a *prereflective web of attitudes, beliefs and response modes.* Until his father died, Colin's family responded to life according to a well-developed, prereflective web of attitudes, beliefs, and response modes. These included parental commitment to spend significant time with their children, a spiritual home environment, clear norms for children's behavior, work-related decisions based on family priorities, and Sunday rituals of church attendance and fun.

The family rarely alluded to such dispositions. They surfaced, however, when something occurred that troubled them, like the evening Colin's father failed to come home at his regular time. Family members became worried, not realizing he had had a flat tire and couldn't get to a phone.

Such a web of attitudes, beliefs, and response modes sprang from mythical patterns established through living in certain ways. The dispositions operative in Colin's family illustrate basic dynamics operative in groups as varied as business offices or church choirs.

*Flowing from a group's mythos, which underlie fundamen-
tal ways in which a group or individuals within the group
approach issues . . . .* Colin's family developed their *presumed
dispositions* in flesh-and-blood experiences with one another.
Parental values, attitudes, and activities set the stage for
development of the family mythos. This mythos in turn rooted
the presumed dispositions that influenced family responses.

The same dynamics that underpinned their presumed dispositions are applicable to any group. A corporate mythos
that holds customers and employees in high regard leads to
better quality merchandise at fair prices and more stringent
safety precautions for employees. Such a mythos often
includes hospitality toward visitors, guests, staff, and customers. It allows customers and employees to be confident
that whenever they deal with this company, these presumed
dispositions will be present. When they are not, people
inevitably wonder why.

In contrast, a selfish, impersonal business mythos often
causes customers and employees instinctively to look over
their shoulders to make sure they are not cheated. The presumed dispositions coming from this corporate mythos are
different from those in the business where hospitality, customer satisfaction, and employee well-being are paramount.

*Approach issues, plan action strategies, and respond ritual-
istically to life situations.* Before Colin's father died, the family
mythos established a prereflective web of presumed dispositions that underpinned fundamental ways family members
related to one another, relaxed on weekends, selected new
clothes for Christmas, and visited neighbors.

Instances showing the influence of presumed dispositions
differ widely. Every club, from a health spa to a Moose Lodge,
has a mythos, which gives purpose to the group. Members
respond to this mythos through prereflective patterns or presumed dispositions. These influence how they deal with
issues, strategize, and respond.

Clubs originally established for men only shifted focus
when women's rights legislation took shape. When this hap-

pened, the mythos of the "men's" clubs changed. So did the presumed dispositions of male club members, who had to deal with womens' issues.

When a mythos changes, so do presumed dispositions. As aspects of the old mythos come to consciousness, they often lose power. Today, recalling unjust treatment of blacks or women in previous generations, we wonder how such injustices were tolerated. The presumed dispositions that once allowed such injustices to happen have no place in today's mythos.

——————— Adaptations to Mythical Change ———————

After Colin's father died, the family's orientation to one another, neighbors, and activities beyond the home changed. Colin's mother found full-time employment outside their home; family members had less time for Sunday outings; and financial hardships ended their vacations. Their old mythos could not deal with the new circumstances.

Contrasted to the *sudden* mythical change in Colin's family, the mythos of women's role in United States society changed *gradually* during the past century. Prior to 1950, few women attended college. Instead, they usually got a job after high school and married in their early twenties. Society's mythos often regarded them as subservient to men. This attitude changed in the latter part of this century.

As the mythos regarding women shifted focus, society adapted. Most contemporary female high school graduates attend college. Women exercise leadership roles in business, religion, and politics. Movements toward inclusive language, equal employment opportunities, and shared parental responsibilities indicate the influence of the current mythos on women's roles.

To clarify the relationship between a shifting mythos and its impact on social patterns, it helps to consider secondary, primary, and core mythic meaning. If a mythos changes, these are affected.

When activities, structures, or organizations change, *secondary mythic meaning* may no longer be realized within the new mythos. Consider Jim's story. He found personal and professional satisfaction in teaching high school for fifteen years. His income provided an adequate livelihood for himself and his elderly mother.

Because unanticipated bills depleted his savings, Jim's teaching salary was insufficient to meet his financial obligations. The secondary mythic meaning he found in his teaching salary lost its significance. Reluctantly, he left this job and entered a new profession that afforded necessary income to satisfy his obligations.

Something similar often happens in business. In my childhood and early adulthood, our dry goods store provided a good income for us and my uncle's family. During this time, society's mythos supported neighborhood stores, for people often lived, shopped, and celebrated in closely knit geographical areas.

About the time Dad retired, the neighborhood store mythos changed. It became harder for small businesses to survive in an atmosphere of rapid transportation and discount stores. Many smaller stores went out of business, unable to compete with large discount stores. When this happened, the income from smaller stores no longer provided secondary mythic meaning for their owners.

Today a significant mythical change happens in large corporations that are forced to downsize. As the computer age intensifies, organizational structures that once provided secondary mythic meaning to companies or individuals become inadequate. When this happens, corporations, workers, and managers adjust or cease to function effectively.

Changes in *primary mythic meaning* also require adaptation. A changing mythos leads to alterations in life patterns, since ways of relating that once afforded primary mythic meaning no longer suffice.

In Colin's case, family relational patterns ceased providing primary mythic meaning after his father died. The family had to adjust rather than live in the past. Something similar may happen after a divorce, as family relational patterns shift. The same applies, as young adults leave home for college.

Changes involving *core mythic meaning* touch deep aspects of human becoming, illustrated by Shelly's story.

Shelly was a free spirit until her early twenties. Some people described her as a wild, spoiled, rich kid. She appeared to care only about herself.

One day, she totaled her motorcycle and was partially paralyzed. Shelly's injuries left her an invalid for several years. Many of her friends didn't come around anymore, and she spent long days by herself.

During her rehabilitation, Edna, an older hospital volunteer, befriended her. They laughed, cried, and talked for hours, often about God, whom Shelly never before considered important. These conversations changed Shelly. What she once valued as important became insignificant in light of the loving God she discovered through Edna.

Today Shelly works with destitute people in a social service agency. No one would recognize the wild, selfish, rich kid, who now dedicates herself to bringing love to neglected people.

During her rehabilitation, Shelly probed the meaning of real happiness. This moved her to reevaluate her life. After she internalized Edna's care and experienced God's love, her core mythos changed. This change affected her values and life-style. Shelly's old ways no longer satisfied her new mythos.

A similar dynamic may occur when an individual or group escapes an oppressive situation. It matters little whether the oppression comes from a hedonistic life-style, an abusive family relationship, or a dysfunctional organization. When people in such situations realize what is happening and strive to overcome their bondage, their core mythic meaning shifts.

————————Dimensions of Mythical Change————————

Social and cultural changes do not follow the laws of logic. They are based, rather, on shifting mythical perspectives. Consequently, every rational analysis of changing social patterns falls short. Using analogies helps to consider such changes. My experiences in an Indiana forest area provide the departure point for such a consideration.

In 1968, I purchased forty-seven acres of heavily wooded forest land in southwestern Indiana. One section, formerly farmed, was now overgrown with briars and small cedar trees. For a year after its purchase, I did little with the land.

In 1969, an automobile accident robbed me of most of my strength. Nothing seemed to help my recovery, and I became progressively weaker. Unable to work and tired of lying around my room, I pushed myself to make the hour-long trip to the Indiana land. With difficulty, I walked amidst the trees, flowers, and briar bushes. An old, broken apple tree, possibly descended from one planted by Johnny Appleseed, became my friend. Its uneven branches symbolized my brokenness. Its courage in adversity symbolized the determination I needed. Identifying with it began my healing process.

When driving my car over the farm field, I could go only a short distance through the briars and grass. A gully between two parts of the property stopped me. I bought a shovel and started to fill in the gully. It took all summer to accomplish this task, but the work strengthened me. Eventually, I drove across the earthen bridge from one field to the next.

In 1970, my strength continued to return. Ironically, as this happened, the old apple tree died. I took its death as a signal to change the contour of the eroded land where it once stood. While I wondered what to do, I received a government notice offering financial assistance to property owners to enable them to build lakes to prevent soil erosion. I applied for funds, got the assistance, and had a lake constructed on the spot where the apple tree once stood.

During the construction, contractors stripped the land and

fashioned a large earthen dam to hold back the water. Con-comitantly, I purchased from the state several hundred white and red pine seedlings to fashion a tree hedge around the lake.

The lake filled in a year, as the surrounding area took new shape. Soon weeds and grass covered the land that had been stripped during the construction. Briars and bushes followed. The pine trees grew as the lake became an integral part of the landscape. Frogs, fish, snakes, rabbits, squirrels, deer, foxes, turkeys, ducks, and coyotes nourished themselves from the water, which was home to water flowers, cattails, algae, and moss. At that point it required considerable work to keep the grass cut around the lake.

Twenty-five years have passed. The pine trees are nearly sixty feet tall. In the lake, large fish jump and frolic. Often I sit by the water, isolated from civilization, reflecting on life's changes. During one such time, I saw how the history of this spot contained basic dimensions of mythical change. I real-ized that mythical change mirrors what happens in nature more than it follows the laws of logic. After all, humans belong to nature. Reflecting on the growth of the area surrounding the lake, four dimensions of mythical change emerged: begin-nings, explorations, dialogue, and maturation.

Beginnings

Before constructing the lake, opportunities for new plants and trees to grow were thwarted by the briars, bushes, and eroded land that covered the open spaces. After the land was stripped and a dam constructed, soil erosion stopped, and the land produced new vegetative forms. When the lake filled, something similar happened in the water as vegetative and animal life began to thrive in a once-barren region.

In watching this process over twenty-five years, I discov-ered that "beginnings" happened not only as the process started but at every progressive stage of growth to maturity.

The process is never static. Some land quickly was covered by trees and shrubs, which kept out the sun's hot rays; other land was not. Where shade predominated, beginnings occurred differently than in sunny areas. In turn, animals began inhabiting one place rather than another. As climate and environment changed, new beginnings continually happened.

The same occurs in any changing mythos. Once a fundamental mythos is established, new beginnings continue to occur, provided the original mythos is maintained. As marriage begins, a couple develops a new mythos, centered on their relationship, work, friends, and children. While they grow together, many starts and stops occur, influenced by various life happenings. If new beginnings cease, the marital relationship fails to grow and the marriage often is in trouble.

During mythical changes, elements formerly held in a group's prereflective awareness burst into consciousness. Insights derived from such awareness combine with the general thrust of the changing mythos to invite new beginnings.

This may happen when a company changes leadership personnel. Take the case of a business office where employees hesitated to speak out because they feared reprisals from their manager. In such a repressive environment, few constructive ideas were expressed. If they were, the manager disregarded them or took it out on the person making the suggestions. Such a mythos did not foster creativity. When a more collaborative manager took over, the mythos shifted. Then the collective wisdom of the employees created fresh opportunities for productive achievement.

Explorations

During the growth of my forest area, some new beginnings materialized, while others did not. Grass, weeds, bushes, and newly planted trees sent out roots and shoots in various directions, searching for water and light. For a while, most of these thrived, as they sought their place in nature's balance. It was almost as if each plant explored its surrounding area, searching for ways to survive.

Something similar happened with the animals. An albino raccoon lived near my toolshed. It became a wonderful addition to the emerging ecological landscape because of its rarity. Unfortunately, this rarity proved its undoing. A predator killed it while it slept, since the raccoon's unusual white coat provided no camouflage. This was not the case with wild turkeys, the forest's most recent addition. They thrive because thick brush behind the lake makes it difficult for humans to detect them. They settled here because the landscape afforded them safety, food, and water.

Something similar happens in changing mythical contexts. When a city's ethnic mix shifts drastically, fundamental mythical patterns change. Just as plants and animals explore various ways to live harmoniously when environmental change occurs, no single model gives the best direction for bringing about harmony in times of racial change. Many starts and stops occur. What works for a while may cease to do so, as the community mythos changes direction.

Usually, different attempts to cope with changing racial situations occur simultaneously, each addressing a different aspect of the shifting mythical pattern. Civic associations, service agencies, churches, governments, and neighborhoods contribute different, yet related pieces to address racial change. Some are more successful than others. Gradually such exploratory efforts solidify as the emerging mythos clarifies.

Dialogue

As the years passed, my forest area and its plant and animal life took definite shape. While some beginnings and explorations continued, the landscape grew into a beautiful harmony where water, trees, bushes, shrubs, insects, fish, and larger animals existed as a living mosaic. Even though this process was interrupted by unusual rainfalls, temperature, or draught, the forest continued to mature in uneven steps.

This regular growth was evident especially in the overnight hours, when I stayed alone in an old trailer on the property. As the forest matured around me, I became a part of the harmony. At dusk, fish in the lake followed me as I walked on the shore. They anticipated food, perhaps sensing that I would not take them from their watery home as my next day's food!

In the summer darkness, night sounds reminded me of my limits. I heard bugs hit my trailer screens in a strange harmony, while the wails of coyotes broke the stillness outside. On every side, bird songs announced their presence. I often walked through the forest at night, guided only by animal sounds and moonlight. During these mystical hours, the entire landscape affirmed its unity and harmony. It seemed as if each part was in dialogue with the whole.

The irregular, yet harmonious growth of the forest pointed to the starts and stops involved in every maturing process. A clear instance of growth happens in a growing friendship. Initially, both parties put their best faces forward. Soon their differences surface as each person learns the other's true self. A developing relationship may be on and off again. During this time, the couple engages in various exploratory efforts, which aim at ascertaining how the other person feels, thinks, acts, and responds.

A growing friendship may require a rearrangement of priorities to give the couple more time to spend together. When friendships continue to grow, real dialogue can begin.

The laity's emergence in the Roman Catholic Church during the past twenty-five years further illustrates the process of dialogical growth.[2] Before that time, the pope, the bishops, and priests exercised church leadership in a closely knit hierarchial institution. Ordination dictated the focus of church ministries, as the clergy regulated church life. Religious men and women taught in Catholic schools and parish religion programs, did hospital work, and performed service functions. Lay people were relegated to a secondary place, with little or no voice in church ministries.

At Vatican II, the mythos grounding the laity's role changed. They soon performed functions once exercised by priests, brothers and sisters. Lay people became distributors of communion to the sick, church readers, counselors for engaged couples, hospital visitors, parish directors of religious education, school principals, and diocesan canon lawyers. As this happened, new beginnings and exploratory efforts occurred, some more successful than others.

This process continues as the church enters a more serious dialogical period between clergy and laity. This is evident where parish teams, commissions, councils, and committees decide on parish priorities and on how to balance lay and clerical responsibilities.[3]

Similar dialogue occurs on national and global levels, as the Catholic Church addresses issues pertaining to world cultures, women, sexual morality, social justice, and economics. This is sometimes accompanied by differing opinions of laity and hierarchy.

The present state of this dialogue indicates that the post–Vatican II church has not yet reached the balance required for mythical maturity. This requires the dialogue to move from the level of rational discourse to a deeper appreciation of the mythical realities involved.

Maturity

Twenty-five years have passed since the seven acres of land surrounding the lake began to take shape. The original two-inch pine trees are now almost sixty feet tall. New plants and animals are regular inhabitants of the forest. At dusk a strange unity exists between the distant pine trees and their reflected images in the crystal-clear lake water. Trees growing side by side blend into one another, especially in the fall, when the contrasting greens of pine trees merge with the reds, browns, and tans of sumac, poplar, maple, persimmon, dog-wood, oak, cherry, locust, and walnut trees. This harmony indicates a maturing forest.

The same thing happens in any mythical emergence. The maturing forest reflects my parents' mature love. Before they married, Dad captured the beginnings of their love in a series of wonderful black-and-white photographs, taken in the 1920s. While growing up, my brother and sisters sat with Dad and Mom, looking through the old photo books and dis-cussing each picture. During these conversations, we learned about their love.

After Dad's death, Mom and I looked at these old pictures again. She focused intently on a scene two years after their marriage. Mom sat next to a fountain and Dad stood next to her. She said, "Bob, you are in that picture." Puzzled, I replied, "Not me, Mom, that's you, Dad, and your friends." "You are there. Look closely, I am pregnant, carrying you," she responded. Chills ran through me, as I saw the first picture of myself, hidden in my mother's womb. This experience touched a core disposition within me that spoke powerfully about my relationship with my parents and about their rela-tionship with each other.

Through the years, many new beginnings and exploratory efforts happened in my parents' emerging mythos, as they grew in understanding and love. The dialogical phase was manifested in deep commitment to each other and our family. As our family unit grew, their mythos became ours. When Dad was dying, their mature mythos culminated. They sat together for hours, saying little, but communicating at the depths of their being.

The day Dad died, my sister, Mary Ann, and I drove to our family home to break the news to Mom. As she greeted us at the door, we said nothing, but noticed tears flowing down her cheeks. Mom faintly whispered, "Oh, Stanley died." With our arms around her, we led her to the living room couch where she and Dad had always sat. Then Mom lay down, cried, and slept the entire day. Her long agony during Dad's last years

was over. Now she rested. Her presence on the couch symbolized the mature fruits of their lifelong mythos.

Response to Mythical Change

Viewing mythical change from a forest-area perspective
invites comparisons between the shifting landscape and
changing mythical patterns. So far, this section has concen-
trated on what happens *externally* by considering beginnings,
explorations, dialogue, and maturity. During this process,
something else goes on *within* individuals or groups experiencing such changes. Although the analogy with the forest
begins to break down at this point, hints can be found here,
pointing to four aspects *within* the process of mythical change
itself, which are present in both sudden and gradual mythic
change: adulation and fear, identity, orthodoxy and ortho-
praxies, and objectivity.[4]

Adulation and Fear

Early stages of mythical change often bring to the surface
deep energies, feelings, and reactions. As long as the old
mythos predominates, these responses remain in check, but
when change occurs, they become evident.

This happened when the collapse of communism in Russia
and Eastern bloc countries released powerful energies. Some
people had the courage and enthusiasm to put their lives on
the line for freedom. At the same time, the changing situation
brought concern about their future.

Something similar happens when a growing relationship
between a man and woman brings new energies, hopes, aspirations, and concerns. As their individual mythos shifts, they
explore future possibilities that may lead to marriage. Likewise, freshmen college students exhibit exuberance, yet
uncertainty, as they adjust to living away from their families

for the first time. Strong emotions accompany their shifting mythical perspectives.

People react differently to new beginnings. Some respond in positive ways, embracing the new energies coming from mythical changes. The energetic response of Russian people at the overthrow of communism, the dreamy eye response of new love, and the enthusiastic reaction of college freshmen indicate how new beginnings bring hope and life.

Other people respond to changes differently, taking a more cautious, fearful approach. Many Russians wondered what the communist overthrow would mean for their survival. The same applies when a newly found love relationship threatens the more independent life-style an individual once enjoyed. Some college students, uncomfortable with their newfound freedom, recoil at this more carefree lifestyle. Such positive and negative reactions occur during all significant life changes.

Adulation and fear are present in times of rapid and gradual change. They manifest themselves at special moments, like anniversaries, birthdays, and holidays. Initial energies, feelings, and reactions inevitably subside, as individuals and groups sort out the implications of change. When this happens, the identity factor enters the picture.

Identity

The questions, Who am I? or Who are we? root our life quest. Coming to grips with them is a slow process. We address such questions during dramatic and gradual change in our never-ending quest for identity.[5] A relatively closed society, like the Communist system, keeps the identity question under constraint. Hence, it is not asked consciously by most individuals or groups.

The Marxist government prevented the ethnic peoples comprising the Soviet Union from celebrating their diversity, since the imposed military mythos guaranteed adherence to the official communist mythos. The latter taught people their identity, as it was ritualized by childhood indoctrination, censorship, suppression of public religious worship, repression, and tight travel controls. As this controlled mythos cracked under a flood of new energy, the identity question emerged. When the Union of Soviet Socialist Republics collapsed, communist military might no longer controlled the governments, peoples, and nations comprising this country. In these uncertain times, many Russian people wondered, Who are we? Initially, this question dwelled in their prereflective awareness. Soon, however, it burst forth into consciousness, as they faced their own identity.

The identity question is asked also by newly married people, as they strive to establish their new role. Functional activities such as career, travel, meetings, and civic responsibilities can affect a couple's efforts to resolve this question. As a marital relationship gradually emerges from the initial reactions of exuberance and fear, this question becomes more pronounced. How a couple addressed it influences their future.

University students also ask the identity question amidst the fun and pressures of college life. They discover new opportunities and encounter unanticipated difficulties, as their developing personalities meet an uncertain, rapidly changing world.

Once a mythos solidifies, identity slips into prereflective awareness, as important mythical elements are taken for granted. They continue, however, to affect peoples' lives.

As the planet moves toward the third millennium, individuals, organizations, and groups face the identity question. Global unification is refocusing the mythoi from which people operate. Dialogue between races, religions, church denominations, sexes, ethnic groups, states, and governments, as well as a better appreciation of the human role in nature's overall plan, promises to reformulate the identity question on a global scale.

Orthodoxy and Orthopraxis

Addressing individual or group identity introduces further questions, such as What do we believe? What do we teach? and How do we act? The first two questions deal with "orthodoxy"; the third one deals with "orthopraxis."[6]

After the Russian revolution, people struggled with norms of belief in the emerging mythos. Many focused on primary dispositions of a religious kind that sprang from their ethnic roots. A religious awakening occurred among Christians, Muslims and other groups. Many religious beliefs supplanted the atheistic creed.

Many Eastern bloc countries, once subsumed under the U.S.S.R. banner, became independent. Mythical changes accompanying this process challenged nations, governments, and individuals to reappropriate core and primary mythic meaning. It also required them to refocus secondary mythic meaning. This meant providing food, shelter, health facilities, governments, civic structures, political processes, and military forces consistent with the new mythos. Further, it required wisdom in coping with huge arsenals of nuclear weapons. Finally, it meant the courage to deal with those loyal to the communist government or with radical, violent forces, intent on taking advantage of the unsettled social condition for personal again.

In such an environment, the questions, What do we believe? What do we teach? and What do we do? have no easy solutions.

Orthodoxy and orthopraxis questions surface in many situations. They occur as a newly married couple faces the future and asks, What do we believe? What do we teach? or How do we act? Some couples deal directly with these questions; others allow them to remain in their unarticulated thoughts and actions. What spouses believe influences their activities. Significant differences between their monetary, social, or religious values can affect their relationship. Spouses who do not face these issues send strong messages to their offspring, for example, when they offer their children no religious upbringing or do not share their personal beliefs with them. These actions send a negative signal about religion's importance in personal and family life. Many college students with no religious upbringing, when learning of their classmates' religious formation, say they were cheated. Many young adults struggle to identify what to believe and teach their children. They also strive to clarify their values, so that their actions are consistent with them. In this process, they sift out their values in light of their mythos.

Orthodoxy and orthopraxis become difficult when individuals, groups, or societies are not sure of who they are. Consequently, their search for central beliefs, right teaching, and consistent modes of action rooted in stable core values remains tentative as they move into the new millennium.

Mythical change brings variations in orthodoxy and orthopraxis. The more stable an individual or group, the less likely it is that major shifts in basic beliefs and actions will occur. It is easier to cope with change if core and primary mythical meaning is established.[7] As a mythos shifts, secondary mythic meaning changes. Then new functional issues emerge that relate to the aspect of objectification.

Objectification

Objectification means putting the consequences of mythic change into viable structures.[8] Like all aspects of change, objectification happens in uneven steps, as old structures disappear and new ones develop. Often new structures are put into place before anyone knows which ones are best. Once established, structures are difficult to change as better ones emerge.

The objectification process comes into play when a mythos changes. This can happen in the changing context of a business, where the old mythos fails to address demands of changing times. Then new functional means are needed to incorporate the company's emerging mythos into workable structures. These means may include setting new goals and objectives, developing organizational strategies, and shifting employee responsibilities to accomplish the company's intended purpose. A changing corporate mythos may require downsizing, expansion into new markets, product specification, or salary freezes. For maximum results, effective objectification needs to produce a delivery system for the goals and objectives dictated by the new mythos.

Objectification is not limited to the corporate world. In one form or another, it applies whenever an individual or group mythos changes. Such change implies a close connection between the ultimate and functional.

The Russian revolution, which replaced the old communist regime, introduced democracy to the once-totalitarian country. This required changes in functional systems that provided food, security, and shelter. Today the Russian people endeavor to develop a different system, compatible with democratic ways.

What happens after divorce illustrates how an ultimate experience requires changes in functional aspects of the objectification process. As divorce deeply touches people's lives, it shifts functional dimensions of the once-married couple. These may include changing a house title, separating checking accounts, paying alimony, and dividing other property.

Effective objectification requires constant refocusing. When the mythos shifts focus, objective norms initially established to govern a nation or put order into a family need adaptation. The success of the objectification process depends on visionaries, leaders, group managers, workers, and volunteers, each with a functional task to accomplish. Congruence between the mythos and its mode of objectification is necessary for any enterprise to succeed.

8

The Sweat Lodge:
Myths, Meaning, and Ritual Activity

S itting in my automobile, looking at the old savings book, I remembered various ritual activities between my father and me, including visits to the savings association, long hours working in the store, playing ball, and frequent trips to church. These rituals solidified our love and set me on a solid path. They gave me direction, support, and confidence.

The relationship with my family illustrates the close connection between a group's mythos and its ritual expressions. Our family was Catholic, so we celebrated the Catholic mythos through regular ritual activities, like prayer and going to church. The Jewish family living nearby celebrated their mythos by faithfulness to their rituals. Rituals act out a group's mythical perspectives. They may be as diverse as a family's practice of celebrating religious feast days or a country's tradition of driving on the right or left side of the road.

Ritual activities focus on core, primary, or secondary mythic meaning. Some family rituals, like praying together or showing affection, relate to core and primary mythic meaning, whereas dividing work chores between family members is associated with secondary mythic meaning.

This chapter examines the complementary relationship between mythos and rituals. It considers the description of ritual; meaning, myth, and ritual activity; the functions of rituals; and the significance and power of rituals.

113

──────────────Description of Ritual──────────────

Planetary movements, seasons of the year, vegetative growth, and animal communications follow regular patterns. In the widest sense, such ritual activity is linked with nature's physical laws of emergence, development, and survival.[1]

Apart from the question of nature's general patterns, specific ritual activity exists in the animal kingdom. Insects, birds, dogs, cats, and fish engage in various rituals that are evident in a forest area. Animals feed, mate, and compete for territory in regular ritual patterns. These activities are manifested also in the rituals of dogs or other domestic animals.

Before Dad became seriously ill, our pet dog, TuTu, sat on the floor in the kitchen next to Dad's chair during meals. Dad put her food on the floor next to him, and she ate it there. During Dad's final illness he could no longer sit at the kitchen table. Mom brought his food into the living room, where he sat on a soft chair. She also put TuTu's food in the usual place on the kitchen floor. When TuTu saw that my father no longer came to the table, she began to quietly pick up her dog biscuits from the kitchen floor in her mouth, carry them to a rug next to him and drop them on the floor by his chair. There she ate her food.

Regular animal patterns—some innate, others learned—point to deep connections among all aspects of the universe. Such connections bind the cosmos into a unified whole. Within this context, human rituals are vitally important.[2]

Human rituals fall within a ritualizing universe, but transcend it. Their uniqueness follows from the human need to search for and discover core and primary mythic meaning. This allows rituals that center on secondary mythic meaning to take new shape in the human enterprise. The ritual of putting money in a savings account normally involves secondary mythic meaning, but with my old savings account, it reflected something deeper.

By analyzing ultimate and functional rituals, the connection between mythos and rituals that convey core, primary, and secondary mythic meaning becomes clearer. The following episodes situate this analysis of ritual activity.

When I was a boy, Mom taught me how to tie my shoes. For a child of two, this was a formidable task. Again and again I tried. Eventually, I learned her method. Fifty-nine years later, I still tie my shoes the way my mother taught me. At about the same time that Mom taught me how to tie my shoes, she taught me how to make the sign of the cross. I struggled to get this ritual correct. Finally, I learned the right way. I still makes the sign of the cross the way Mom taught me.

Is there a difference between these two rituals? From one point of view, there is little difference. Both require specific, functional skills. They involve repeatable patterns of action, learned at an early age. From another perspective, however, they are far different. Tying my shoes serves a utilitarian purpose: it prevents them from falling off. It has secondary mythic meaning. Someone else may have taught me another way to tie them. Making the sign of the cross is different. Although it involves a functional ritual (secondary mythic meaning), the act is more than functional. It serves no utilitarian purpose but points beyond to an ultimate reality.

When I was a child, the difference between the two rituals was hard for me to appreciate. When I understood the meaning of the sign of the cross, this ritual became evocative, not utilitarian. It opened up deeper vistas, involving faith and belief. Then the sign of the cross ritualized aspects of my core and primary mythic meaning, which transcends the functional act of moving my hands and arms across my body.

Learning this functional ritual in childhood had lasting consequences. Its significance was embedded in my psyche. Since it was important for my mother and father, it became important for me. When I grew up and learned its meaning, this functional activity became ultimately meaningful.

Ritual is a patterned and regular acting out of a mythos that an individual or group has made its own.[3]

Rituals involve *patterned and regularly acted out actions.* Habits are vital to human growth, as they are to all animals. Ritual activity links intimately with such habits. A single action does not qualify as a ritual. The first time Gerry enters a class and sits by the window, she has not established a ritual for herself. If, however, she sits in the same seat every class, her patterned actions become functional rituals.

Jewish worship includes the Sabbath as a holy day. Christians ritualize Sunday as their holy day. Both ritual activities happen in regular and structured ways, flowing from different mythical perspectives. Regularly repeated activities that act out a mythos qualify as rituals. Acting out a mythos may take the form of functional actions, like employees required to work at a definite job task each day. Rituals act out an ultimate mythos through patterned and regular repetitions of more ultimate actions, like spousal love, sibling affection, or religious ceremonies.

The same ritual may act out an aspect of an ultimate or functional mythos. If Joe, a teenage boy, regularly cuts a neighbor's grass for money, this ritual flows from the functional mythos of getting paid for doing a job. In this case, the ritual of cutting the grass is functional. If, however, Joe cuts his mother's grass out of love, the ritual flows from an ultimate mythos. In this case, cutting the grass becomes an ultimate ritual. Hence, the same external action can be ultimate or functional depending on a person's mythos.

Rituals reflect the mythos that *an individual or group has made its own.* Rituals carry out, reinforce, or celebrate a mythos. Loving one's neighbor is central to the Christian mythos. A person who makes this mythos his or her own may ritualize it through volunteer work in a soup kitchen or social service agency.

Since mythical perspectives are vital to us, so are the rituals that externalize them. We take ownership, consciously or unconsciously, of our ritual patterns. One way to upset people is to upset their rituals. An athlete may feel uncomfortable if he or she forgets to wear a special symbol that has brought success in the past. An informal group may be inwardly disturbed if the room assigned for a meeting has immovable chairs, thus giving the gathering a more formal air.

Identifying peoples' ritual patterns enhances better communication. When beginning my work with one Native American group, I was invited to give a weekend seminar to their leaders. Out of deference to me, the only non–Native American present, they arranged the assembly space in traditional classroom style. Upon entering the room, I saw the podium, blackboard, and rows of chairs arranged in hierarchical fashion. Instinctively, I said, "Let's put the chairs in a circle." They enthusiastically responded, and we began the seminar. I never realized the ritual significance they give to the circle, which they regard as a sacred symbol. Sitting in a circular fashion expresses equality among the participants.

In the afternoon, at a ceremonial aspect of the meeting, I again invited them to put a table, necessary for the celebration, into the circle. At that point, a native woman who had not joined us through the whole day entered the room and joined the circle. She and I had extensive conversation through the remaining two days. After the seminar ended, we became good friends.

Several years later, we discussed the first time we met. I asked, "Would you tell me why you never joined the group until the afternoon session? She replied, "I deal with many white people that look down on Native Americans and subtly manipulate us. I didn't know whether or not you were one of them."

"What made you conclude that I was not?" I continued. She answered, "When you moved the table into the ceremonial circle the second time, I knew you were different. Then I knew you regarded us as equals."

Mythos and ritual are intimately related. Together they

fashion living environments where humans pursue meaning, purpose, and fulfillment.

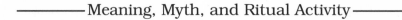

Meaning, Myth, and Ritual Activity

A subsequent experience with Native Americans profoundly influenced my perspective on modes of mythic meaning and the rituals accompanying them. The occasion was my first invitation to participate in the Ojibway Leadership Seminar in Thunder Bay, Ontario, Canada. Shortly after I arrived, Eva, an Ojibway woman, asked me to help her make final arrangements for beginning our journey to the leadership conference. The station wagon was loaded with blankets, shovels, picks, towels, and roles of thick canvaslike cotton material.

After arriving at our destination, we approached a clearing, surrounded by trees. Ojibway elders were fashioning willow trees, cut from the bush, into a dome-shaped structure about eight feet in diameter. At its center, a man dug a pit into which red-hot coals would be placed.

The chief elder asked me to unravel the grey canvaslike cotton material that we had brought in the station wagon. Three layers were wrapped around the firmly tied willow branches, until no light could penetrate inside the sweat lodge. Finally, we put heavy stones around the bottom of the material and fashioned an entrance about thirty inches high, making sure to allow enough material for a flap door. The latter kept light out of the sweat lodge, after it was closed.

During the construction, Ojibway elders explained the meaning of the sweat-lodge ritual. They invited me to participate in the ceremony later that evening. I felt honored, but became troubled after I learned that the sacred pipe was smoked several times after the flap was closed. Since I am allergic to smoke, I feared getting sick if I stayed inside the lodge during the entire ritual. I explained my problem to an elder, expressing a desire to join them but indicating my reluctance to stay in the lodge because of my smoke allergy.

After the elder consulted with other elders, I received their answer. They invited me to follow the ceremony's leader into the sweat lodge as the ritual began and to leave whenever necessary.

We assembled for the sweat after dinner. As the ritual began, the leader walked in a circle, before crawling into the sweat lodge on his knees. He sat on one side of the entrance and invited me to sit on the other, so I could breathe fresh air as long as the entrance was open.

After all were assembled, the leader began the prayers, chants, and blessings. Soon the fire keeper outside put the first white-hot rocks into the center pit with a pitchfork. Sacred water hissed, as it was sprinkled on the hot coals. The vapor emitted hinted at how hot it would become after the flap was closed and sealed from the outside by more large rocks.

Next the leader prepared the pipe, smoked it, and passed it to us. After more chants, sweet grass, water sprinkling, and pipe smoking, it was time to close the flap. From the beginning, the smoke affected me, but sitting near the door, I continued to breathe fresh air. After the flap closed, this would no longer be possible.

Quietly, the leader signaled me, indicating that they were about to close the flap. Knowing I could help outside in preparing the hot rocks, thereby remaining part of the community sweat, I reluctantly crawled outside. The flap was closed and sealed.

I listened attentively to the muffled chants, prayers, and discussions within the lodge. Occasionally, the fire keeper explained what was happening. After about an hour, the leader called for more hot rocks, which we delivered on pitchforks and laid in the center pit.

On two separate occasions, the participants came out to get air, before returning. At 2:20 A.M. the ritual ended. It had lasted over three hours. During that time, we had put seventeen massive hot rocks inside the sweat lodge.

For quite a while, steam continued to pour from the bodies of those attending the full sweat. After they cooled off, we celebrated with food, drink, and laughter. Then we returned to our sleeping quarters to await the dawn.

I experienced various modes of mythic meaning, as we ritualized the mythos surrounding the sweat lodge. This experience gave me new awareness of how mythos, meaning, and rituals interact on different levels.

Rituals and Core Mythic Meaning

Through this ritual, I felt a powerful sense of *core mythic meaning*. This feeling drew me beyond myself into a realm of mystery and meaning that transcended my senses. It began as we journeyed to the sweat lodge, continued in its construction, intensified when I entered it, and culminated outside, as I contributed to the ritual within the lodge.

The ritual's power comes from a fundamental experience within the Native American community, whose mythos grounds the ritual. It intensifies through the place, space, music, songs, and seriousness of the specific Native American group that celebrates it. My experience related life's meaning with the earth and with these Ojibway people that I barely knew. We connected in our common humanity.

Seeing the sparks of light coming from the hot rocks sprinkled with sacred water, smelling the tobacco smell from the sacred pipe, and feeling the sweat pour from my body brought me into an encounter with a transcendent reality. The primordial dynamism flowing through this experience reinforced my meaning, roots, and connections by opening up a realm of existence that went beyond the assembled people, earth, air, fire, and water. It evoked from my spiritual core feelings of my limits, yet expressions of my worth in the cosmic enterprise.

Mystery surrounded these rituals. The sweat lodge linked me with earth, plants, animals, and people, while rooting me in a cosmic dimension where God dwells. It spoke of solidarity with a spiritual world, while affirming human brokenness and the need for healing. It helped me let go of my hurts, seek forgiveness, and be at peace.

During the ceremony, the intense heat felt by those within the lodge, coupled with personal sharing, initiates a reconciliation process. Analogies with the Catholic ritual of confession are striking. Participants' discussions are kept in absolute confidence, similar to the secrecy required of the priest in the Catholic rite. Purification through heat symbolizes the discipline needed to let go of past hurts and be reconciled. The personal dimension of the ritual evokes primary mythic meaning.

The ritual operated in a milieu deeper than social analysis, psychology, or psychiatry can touch. It invited me to reexamine how secular rituals often canonize noise, flee solitude, functionalize superficiality, and lack dynamism. In so doing, they often fail to touch core mythic meaning.

The relationship between core mythic meaning and ritual activities has implications for our churches. Current disenfranchisement with organized religion often results because church rituals fail to touch this level of core mythic meaning. Something similar can happen in families. Divorce, neglect, abuse, drugs, and alcohol, as well as substitute satisfactions sought from money, pleasure, and position, challenge Western society to create environments conducive to family rituals rooted in core mythic meaning.

The mythos of many churches and families, however, includes transcendent qualities such as love, support, respect, and reconciliation. When these are present, rituals of work, recreation, prayer, religious practices, and social activities bear rich fruit.

Rituals and Primary Mythic Meaning

My experiences of primary mythic meaning came in the welcome and invitation of the Ojibway leaders to participate in the sweat lodge ritual. During my time with them, I realized the close connection between a community's mythos and its rituals. No matter how I tried, I could not appreciate what really happened in this ritual. Its full meaning depended on their cultural mythos, much of which eluded me.

I understood the ceremony from the mode of core mythic meaning and from their explanations (secondary mythic meaning). To internalize how their mythos and ritual activity connected required more. This "more" makes it difficult for someone outside of a culture to understand another culture's primary mythic meaning.

While standing in the cold, thirty-seven-degree temperature, next to the fire, I thought, "If only I experienced the sweat once, I would have a better sense of its meaning." But even if I was inside, I couldn't understand this ritual's full cultural mythic meaning. It is embedded in the mythos of the Ojibway people.

Primary mythic meaning addresses personal and cultural bonds that transcend specific differences within cultural groups. The Ojibway community, assembled for the sweat, came from various villages. The leader was unknown to many participants. He performed the ceremonies differently from the way other elders did it. How he ritualized this ceremony wasn't the issue. How it inspired the participants was. Those present bonded in a ritual that revealed primary mythic meaning, rooted in their mythos as Ojibway people.

Cultural identity alone does not bring primary mythic meaning. Many individuals belonging to the same family or ethnic group fail to communicate. Primary mythic meaning also depends on the quality of personal relationships, which transcend cultures. This happened between the Ojibway leaders and me.

The new millennium challenges various cultures to acknowledge their unique gifts, as they communicate in mutual friendship, respect, and welcome. When this happens, they operate on the level of primary and core meaning.

The need to bridge cultural gaps also challenges our churches. Sometimes they wonder how meaningful rituals can include various age and ethnic groups. If churches address this issue from the perspective of secondary mythic meaning while neglecting deeper modes of core and primary mythic meaning, little can be done. If, however, they relate their ritual activities to peoples' common needs, the same ritual may have deep meaning for various peoples.

Families too are challenged to center their priorities, decisions, and relationships around primary and core mythic meaning. When this happens, basic human needs common to every member establish the norms for family living. Family rituals, suffused with a healthy balance of the functional and ultimate, bring energy and life.

During the leadership conference, I better learned how personal experiences filtered through different cultures bring meaning that transcends ethnic boundaries. The bonding in the sweat lodge sprang from our common humanity. We possessed the same human spirit. We were one as we ritualized core and primary mythic meaning in a structured, yet spontaneous way.

The sweat-lodge ritual blended structure and spontaneity. Since it repeated already known ritual patterns in a structured way, the Ojibway participants felt comfortable. These ritual patterns involved crawling into the lodge, sitting in a circle and using sacred water, sweet grass, cedar, sage, tobacco, and the eagle feather.

Since it allowed for spontaneity, the ritual enabled us to celebrate the special gifts of those present. Hence, it permitted variations in the lodge's size, number of stones used, and time spent inside. Such spontaneity ensures adaptability to circumstances, places, times, and persons. Rituals, however, too strong in spontaneity and lacking in structure, bring confusion, unrest, and ambiguity.

All meaningful rituals include a healthy blend of spontaneity and structure. Overstructured rituals, without spontaneity, soon become ossified, cutting themselves off from their transcendent energy source. Spontaneity without structure leads to chaos. When orderly patterns cease to dictate our responses, we become confused and lose focus.

Rituals and Secondary Mythic Meaning

My experience of the sweat-lodge ritual also had secondary mythic meaning for me. This centered on learning about this ritual. Being there taught me more about it than I had learned in academic studies (secondary mythic meaning).

My learning began as the elders instructed me about the sweat lodge's origin, history, and procedures and as the fire keeper continued this explanation after I left the lodge. Their words had secondary mythic meaning for me. Now I can explain what I learned to others. Experiences of core and primary mythic meaning, which happened inside the lodge, can be described, but only in a limited way.

The ritual also had secondary mythic meaning for the Ojibway leaders. While they knew its origin and history, its well-executed functional aspects allowed them to experience core and primary mythic meaning.

This ritual contrasts with many Western rituals which stress secondary mythic meaning. These may include written contracts, tight schedules, specific accountability procedures, organized child care, rushed shopping, filing reports, paying bills, and household chores. Many of these rituals are necessary. They present challenges, however, when they sap the spontaneity and zest out of life. When this happens, society's functionalization affects core and primary mythic meaning.

The new millennium challenges us to consider what happens when we substitute functional rituals that afford secondary mythic meaning for those that bring core and primary mythic meaning.

─────────────── Functions of Rituals ───────────────

Personal trauma, such as a child's death or a divorce, and *social* upheaval, such as wars or earthquakes, shake peoples' identity. At such times, old ritual patterns collapse and new ones develop. In light of such experiences, theologian Hans Mol says, "Rituals articulate and reiterate a system of meaning. . . . They restore, reinforce, or redirect identity."[5] The story of a young married couple reflects how rituals root, order, change, and transcend life.

Shops and entertainment complexes filled the small resort town where Mom and I vacationed. One afternoon, we drove past a plethora of mega-shopping malls, boutiques, restaurants, variety shops, and festivals. As we looked at the endless variety of junk products amidst quality merchandise, I said, "Mom, this town is one big flea market."

Like most tourists, we looked through the shops for a memorable souvenir of our visit. Eventually, Mom and I walked to the end of the shops to use the bathroom. While she went inside, I waited outside. I spotted a man facing the spot where the bathroom ended and the forest began. Here a beautiful panorama of pine trees introduced visitors to the fantastic landscape beyond. As the man turned, I noticed he wore a black tuxedo, which was strangely out of place in this tourist mecca. Then, I recalled seeing a sign advertising a second-floor wedding chapel over a boutique shop.

I said, "Are you going to get . . . ?" The young man smiled nervously and blurted out, "No, just got married." As he began speaking, a woman wearing a white wedding dress came from the bathroom and joined him. I congratulated them. The man replied, "This is our first marriage."

Somewhat surprised that this was his first complete sentence, I continued, "That's great! I hope you have such a wonderful married life that it is your last marriage." My remark triggered an emotional reaction in them. Apparently, they were jolted into a new realization of what had just happened in the wedding chapel.

The man's jaw twitched, as he answered, "Yes, that's right! I sure hope so. We want that." The man's and woman's nods and smiles indicated that my words touched a deep core within them. With grateful hearts, they joined hands and thanked me. I wished them happiness, love, and God's blessing. Soon they disappeared into the crowd.

To my knowledge, I was the only person besides the wedding magistrate and witnesses to congratulate them. It seemed as if they first realized in our conversation that they had begun a sacred journey, something more important than buying a product in one of the shops near the wedding chapel, which could be discarded later when it was outdated. At that moment, they saw that their marriage was more than a civil ritual to satisfy a legal obligation.

This episode provides a point of departure for considering the functions of rituals, which root, order, change, and transcend life.

All rituals *root* life in some way. The young couple's marriage, no matter how they celebrated it, set their life on a new path. It challenged them to move the focus of their identity from each one alone to include their spouse.

They officially began this rooting process through the wedding-chapel ritual before a civil magistrate, with a stranger's congratulations, in a vacation area. Regardless of circumstances, this ritual rooted unknown possibilities for what their married life might become. This rooting process can be centered on ultimate or functional values.

Every significant ritual helps to establish a person's identity within a group. This rooting process initiates new behavior patterns or reinforces old ones, as in the case of a person who is hired by a company. The employee's contract links the person with the company, spelling out responsibilities and obligations. This initial linking is ritualized further by the welcome received from other employees and managers. Subsequent promotions, salary increases, and bonuses reinforce this identity.

Ultimate rituals play a more inclusive role in the rooting process. They link people with the earth, another person, or a community. Native American rituals, like the sweat lodge, join the participants with the earth. So do cultures that ask for

God's blessing on the spring crop plantings or give thanks for the fall harvest. Birthing rituals, preparing the home, and nursing ritualize a child's entrance into the world while anticipating the child's welcome into the family.

Christian baptism roots a person within a specific religious community. Something similar happens in the initiation rites employed by various church or social groups. Such rituals go beyond the functional and establish the groundwork for bonding with the particular group.

Ultimate rituals touch core and primary mythic meaning. In so doing, they link us with a larger community. Celebrations, like Memorial Day ceremonies, join community members with brave men and women who gave their lives so that United States citizens might be free. Such rituals enhance our individual and social identity.

Besides rooting life, rituals establish parameters to *order* our activities. In the wedding chapel, the married couple changed the style of their individual lives. A new direction began, as they set out on a path which affected their personal, social, and professional obligations.

Ritual patterns give order to families, churches, social agencies, and everyday life. Family rituals dictate meal times, responsibilities for chores, procedures to share money, and ways to locate loved ones in an emergency. In everyday life, we stop at red lights, drive on the right side of the road, pay taxes, and fulfill functional obligations according to predetermined rituals. Failure to do so disrupts our lives. Church members celebrate religious beliefs through specific ritual activities. Jews gather to praise God on the Sabbath, Christians on Sunday. During worship services, we sit, stand, and kneel in definite patterns.

A ritual establishes social and psychological stability by providing a sense of "being at home." We are comfortable when we experience regularly repeated rituals. Such rituals alleviate anxiety and provide comfort in tense situations.

Strangers in unfamiliar settings often feel lost, because the rituals they experience are unknown to them.

We perform many rituals as a matter of course, like getting up in the morning, driving to work, or eating lunch. When our rituals are upset, we get upset, since they give us security. Rituals establish the structure necessary for us to respond according to expected patterns.

During times of *change and transformation,* we celebrate key life moments with rituals of passage, including birth, sickness, and death. Rites of passage also are associated with change of lifestyle, for example, entering a religious community, getting married, obtaining a divorce, going into the military, or graduating from school.[6]

Some life experiences that bring about life change can be anticipated; others cannot. Both involve significant rites of passage. Anticipated life moments may include birth, beginning school, getting as driver's license, graduating, celebrating marriage, or entering the armed services. Rituals supporting people in such circumstances can be pre-planned.[7]

Some life changes cannot be anticipated. These may include suffering, job loss, spousal infidelity, property destruction, unexpected job promotions, winning the lottery, unexpected pregnancy, or sudden death. Such unanticipated life happenings often leave us bewildered, angry, and confused. Rituals to deal with such experiences often cannot be pre-planned. At such times, family members, friends, social agencies, neighborhood groups, church communities, and business associates can afford great support.

Finally, rituals help us *transcend* the functional and move to deeper life dimensions. While functional and ultimate rituals root, order, and change life, the transcending function of rituals is limited to ultimate rituals. Ultimate rituals liberate us from secular bonds and deepen our commitment to basic values. After my conversation with the young married couple, they saw a deeper significance to their marriage. This went beyond the functional trappings of a secular event. Watching them disappear into the crowd reminded me of the day that I found a nicely bound, handmade book in a flea market.

It was a wedding book, which the groom's friend had put together for this newly married couple. Every saying and anecdote interspersed between pictures of the couple's recent wedding was blatantly secular. Such comments abounded: "May life bring you success and fame!" "May you rise to the top in your professions!" "May you be millionaires before you are thirty!" The final words in the book read, "Cherish this token as a symbol of what is really important for a successful marriage." A quarter was pasted in the center of the page. The marriage probably failed, and that's probably the reason the book ended up on a flea market stand. It had a price tag of twenty-five cents. How ironic that the quarter that was to symbolize success in their marriage was the exact cost of the book at the flea market.

Functional actions alone cannot sustain life's deep challenges. But ultimate rituals, like praying, comforting a loved one, sacrificing for friends, and receiving support, transcend the secular and lead us to real freedom.

In painful situations, ultimate rituals offer us hope. During an intense sickness years ago, the presence of my family and friends encouraged me to hope for eventual liberation from my pain. During this time, religious rituals reminded me of Jesus in his suffering. Often, while alone, I looked at the crucifix and thought, "If you could endure it, so can I. Give me strength." This ritual helped me survive the pain that engulfed my body and provided a doorway into a transcendent realm that became most real for me. Here I saw the limits of the secular and the liberating power of the transcendent.[8] Entering this transcendent realm through ritual activity deepens our lives and enables us to focus better on what is really important. Then we understand that there is never enough time for everything, but plenty of time for what is really important.

─────── The Significance and Power of Rituals ───────

A ritual's significance varies depending on whether it is functional or ultimate. Functional rituals, like those associated with shopping, cleaning, working, managing an office, or organizing a meeting, derive significance from their role in fulfilling personal or organizational goals.

A generation ago, to drive an automobile often meant learning the ritual movements associated with shifting into various gears. When automatic transmissions became popular, such skills were no longer needed. The ritual ability to drive a stick shift automobile has little significance today.

Office managers formerly analyzed employee reports, recorded hours worked, and calculated salaries. Today computers perform many of these tasks. Functional rituals become obsolete when the activity changes or no longer serves the group's goals.

More ultimate rituals, like affirming a spouse's love or celebrating a community belief, lose their significance when the mythos is not consistent with the rituals. This may happen if a woman learns her husband is involved with another person, but continues to show her affection. When the mythos that originally solidified their relationship changed, his ritual actions of pretending that he still loves her become a lie.

A close relationship exists between a ritual's significance and its power. Rituals gain or lose power in relation to the mythos that influences them. When a mythos changes, adaptations are necessary if the ritual is to continue to have its intended effect.

Problems arose in an insurance company's branch offices located throughout the United States. An outdated computer system made it increasingly difficult to guarantee prompt claim payments. After an employee developed a unified ritual system for the organization, the company installed it. This system incorporated new ritual patterns that adequately fulfilled the company's mythos.

When I was young, Sundays were special. After church and lunch, our family took an afternoon ride or went to a park for a picnic. We spent our time in fun and relaxation. These outings continued until I was in high school. Then they became less frequent, as I developed new interests. As my childhood mythos shifted focus, the Sunday rituals lost some of their power. New ones took their place, as our family developed more flexible ways to share our love.

Rituals are vital in our quest for meaning. Closely associated with mythic meaning, they are important pathways on life's journey.

9

The Old Wooden Chairs: Symbols—Unlocking Life's Meaning

The old savings book had deep significance because it symbolized the relationship with my father. This became evident while I sat at the stop sign before proceeding to the Centennial Savings Bank to close the account. The age-worn three-by-five-inch book made actual the love between my father and me.

The savings book provides the point of departure for considering symbols. Symbolic activity is a unique mode of communication, which distinguishes humans from other animals. It enables us to probe the cosmic mystery, inviting us to search for life's meaning and to link present actions and future hopes with core dispositions, which provide the fundamental blueprint for a happy life.

Modern society stands at a crossroad, as various cultures intersect. While different mythical perspectives come together, a shift occurs in symbolic activities, including language and ways of acting. To move confidently into this new era, it helps to appreciate better the ways that symbols work.

This chapter considers the relationship between symbols and meaning; symbols and signs; the revelatory aspects of symbols; and symbols, context, and meaning.

————————— Symbols and Meaning —————————

Cool fall days are a good time to attend farm auctions. Hospitality is more evident as farmers relax after a hard summer. The temperature allows unfettered discussions to stretch out the homespun tales that are part and parcel of country gettogethers. On one such day, I attended a farm auction near my Indiana property. Tony, the old farmer whose farm and possessions were on the auction block, had died some months earlier, and his wife could not keep up the place.

As I trudged up the long, winding gravel farm road from the highway to Tony's farmhouse, I thought of him. He had never mentioned his background, except what he told me about his wonderful wife and children. His sons and daughters had left the farm when they went off to college. Only he and his wife remained in the homestead.

The auction had already started as I came to the brow of the hill and saw the farmhouse. The tractors and large farm equipment had already been sold, and the lunch provided by the local Baptist church was nearly gone. Most people stood or sat with friends in different parts of the farm, examining small auction items on tables or larger ones in clusters around the property.

A flatbed wagon contained small vases, pictures, clocks, and coins. As I walked around the wagon, I noticed four elderly farmers, whose bidding was over once the barn contents were auctioned off. They sat in old chairs under a big oak tree with fall breezes and cool drinks adding enjoyment to their hospitable conversation.

The men, friends of mine, signaled for me to join them. We laughed and reminisced for about half an hour. Then the auctioneer approached. As he did, I moved aside, but the four old men kept sitting on the chairs, which were now on the auction block.

I looked more closely at the backs, arms, and sides of the chairs, which the men continued to occupy. The chairs were very old, hand-cut out of barrel staves with high arms and deep backs, conducive to rest and relaxation. "Someone," I thought, "went to great pains in making them."

The auctioneer began the bidding, while the men remained sitting in the chairs. He started, "Here we have four old chairs, handmade out of barrel staves. Who will bid $25.00." No answer. The auctioneer continued, "No takers? I'll throw in the old men. Who will give me $10.00?" No takers. He continued, "What will someone bid?" Sheepishly, I said, "One dollar." "I've got a dollar for the four chairs. Anyone bid two?" No one answered. "Sold, for one dollar!" he said.

As the auction wound down, I gathered together my purchases and prepared to leave. I planned to tie the chairs on my Jeep truck and take them to my farm.

I approached the farmers, who were still sitting on them, and mentioned that I was leaving. They smiled and said, "Bob, we're going to sit a spell more. Anyway, you'd have a hard time getting these chairs on your truck. Leave them here and we'll drop them at your place." I said fine, and started down the farm path to the highway.

I had walked just a few yards, when I heard someone struggling to keep up with me. Turning around, I saw an elderly woman with a cane, who asked me to stop. She said, "You bought the old chairs, made from the whiskey barrels, didn't you?" "Yes," I replied. "Will you take them to your place?" she continued. I explained that the farmers were to bring them to my farm.

With that, she cried and said,

I thought so. I heard you talking to Tony's friends before you left. I didn't know until that time who bought the chairs. It was too painful to watch them go, when they were auctioned off. I'm glad someone nice got them. Even though we never met, I know who you are, because Tony told me about you.

My name is Bertha and Tony was my husband. I wanted to keep the farm, but it was too much work. My arthritis makes it difficult to walk and take care of myself.

Next week I go into a retirement home. It was hard seeing all these precious memories of my lifetime going to other people who do not know their significance. Do you understand?

I told her I sensed how hard it must be for her to leave. As Bertha became more comfortable with me, she continued,

The hardest thing about this auction is parting with the four chairs that you bought. Shortly after we were married, Tony spent months cutting, carving, and fashioning those chairs from oak barrels. He made them strong and comfortable. They were his present to me on the first Christmas we were married. It's all he could afford; during the Depression, we were lucky to have food to eat.

Before he finished them, I became pregnant with our first child. When spring came, Tony placed them on the front porch of the farmhouse. They sat there for fifty years, until the auctioneer removed them today.

The chairs know the history of our family and this farm. During good times, Tony and I laughed and celebrated on them; In hard times we sat on them, crying, praying, and asking God for strength. When our children came, I nursed them, taught them about God, and encouraged them to be good on these chairs.

The four chairs witnessed family gatherings, childhood play, deer in the fields, and weddings. Hot summer evenings found Tony and me sitting on them, praying for rain on our wilting crops. We relaxed on these chairs during the cool fall evenings, rejuvenating ourselves after a long day. Here we saw the winter snow fly and the spring buds, which invited rabbits and squirrels to play once more in the meadows.

These chairs symbolize my life story. As I leave this farm, they also must go. I wanted to tell you something about their history. When you enjoy them, remember Tony, me, my family, and the old farm. I'd do the same for you.

As Bertha walked back toward the house and I moved toward the highway, tears covered our faces. We shared a profound moment, when the old oak chairs evoked memories of Tony's, his wife's, and their children's passage along life's journey. I was honored to join Bertha during this final day at the farm. A week later, I entered my farm gate and the old wooden chairs awaited me.

The story of the old wooden chairs illustrates the way symbols touch the depths of human meaning. They carry power that focuses significant events, persons, and places. Things often assume symbolic power because they connect with important experiences or events in our lives. In themselves, the oak chairs were only things. Before I knew their history, the oak chairs' import as symbols was unknown to me. They assumed symbolic importance because of their history.

Tony had made these chairs for Bertha. She recalled their place through her past memories. The experiences they symbolized were ritual activities that charged the chairs with symbolic power.

Symbolic actions and the things they symbolize depend on more fundamental life dimensions, rooted in our mythos and rituals. Just as a relationship exists between mythos and rituals, so do mythos and rituals influence a symbol's significance. The old chairs had great significance for Bertha, because the family's mythos and ritual activities filled her with meaning. The chairs were a capsulized summary of her family's life on the farm.

Before Bertha told me their story, the chairs had no symbolic value to me. I bought them for a functional purpose. Their symbolic power clarified during our conversation. What were previously "things" became symbols of a loving family.

Symbols, like the wooden chairs or the old savings book, make concrete the deep dynamics present in a mythos. They are pointers saying to those involved, "Look! Something very important is symbolized."

———————— Symbols and Signs ————————

Humans and other animals use symbols, but not in the same way.[1] Symbolic actions of animals are directed primarily by instinct. Rational reflection, as in human thought processes, is unknown to them.

Human survival depends on our unique ability to use symbols. This enables us to write, speak, keep historical records, think abstractly, share emotions, praise God, express insights, build homes, construct bridges, and program computers. Symbolic activity also allows us to develop mythical patterns and give ritual responses to innate urges coming from our core dispositions.

Symbols take different shapes and tones depending on their use in human discourse. The complex nature of human communication hints at the complexity of symbolic activity that makes such communication possible. The terms "symbols" and "signs" often are used interchangeably, but they refer to different realities.

Signs imply something functional. They derive their meaning from custom or designation by a group, community, or nation. A red light tells a driver to stop, whereas a green one means the individual can proceed. Signs can be interpreted in only one way by those who understand them.

Typed letters on a computer keyboard are sign functions. Each letter must be typed exactly, or the word becomes garbled. The same applies when a writer saves a document on a word processing program. The software requires that we follow an exact series of instructions. Each step must be performed exactly to get the correct results.

Symbols differ from signs in that symbols are most closely associated with the ultimate, while signs relate to the functional. For Bertha, the chairs were symbols that touched an ultimate part of her life. It was different with me. I bought them, figuring they would be functional additions on my farm. Before Bertha and I spoke, they signified a good purchase. Afterwards, they took on symbolic importance.

Symbols, while relating to ultimate dimensions of life's meaning, touch deep aspects of the whole person.

A symbol is an action or a thing that attempts to realize through concrete expression some ultimate aspect of human

becoming and derives its dynamism from fundamental rela-
tions upon which human experience is founded.

An action or thing that attempts to realize through concrete
expression. A symbol's significance is rooted in relationships.
Human actions involve relational patterns with the universe,
earth, plants, animals, and other humans. Communication
with other people is of special importance. The wooden chairs
symbolized the loving relationships that framed the mythos
between Tony, Bertha, and their family. A lifetime of love, concern, and sacrifice was captured in the symbolic power of
these chairs.

Symbols are concrete expressions of something more. They
capture in themselves the significance of multiple relational
patterns existing between persons.

Some aspect of human becoming. Because the old chairs
symbolized loving moments and difficult times, it was hard for
Bertha to part with them. The chairs served as a moving picture, capturing specific moments that rooted this family's
meaning structure. Letting them go was saying goodbye to a
meaningful part of Bertha's life.

The chairs were culturally produced symbols. Bertha's
family culture and experiences gave them meaning and purpose. Natural symbols, like fire and water, belong to another
classification. Unlike the chairs, they have a built-in capacity
to symbolize universal dimensions of human becoming.

Many rituals, like Christian baptism and Buddhist purification ceremonies, employ natural symbols. Although differing in mythical perspectives, these rituals are meaningful for
Christians and Buddhists, because the water symbolizes the
life-and-death dimensions inherent throughout the universe.

Derives its dynamism from fundamental relations upon
which human experienced is founded. Bertha's sorrow in seeing the old chairs leave her farm indicates that some actions
touch core dispositions more deeply than others. The chairs
symbolized her love for Tony and her family. They evoked a
fundamental meaning that reached the core of her being. The
chairs had the power to trigger this response, because their

symbolic significance was rooted in the life–death dynamism that underlies all life experiences.

Living in close proximity to the earth, Bertha knew that life must change but is never ended. She learned this from nature's life–death–resurrection patterns. She realized it first-hand as Tony died and she moved to the retirement home.

The death of a family member, friend, or admired person triggers within us a similar yearning. It reminds us of death's reality and moves us to hope that death is but a passage into new life.

Core dispositions urge us to yearn for a better life beyond the grave. Religious myths, promising life after death, hold out such a hope for humankind.[2] Belief in the Native American Happy Hunting Ground, Hindu reincarnation, and Christian resurrection, touch core dispositions, energize people, and give them hope.

Symbols can be classified as natural and culturally produced symbols. Their difference lies in whether they relate to core dispositions naturally or through cultural expressions.

Natural symbols, like the circle, water, or fire, take their ultimate dynamism from patterns inherent in the universe. The *circle*, a natural symbol of wholeness, is found throughout the universe. The yearly seasons, lunar cycles, vegetative and human growth patterns, and planetary shapes reflect the natural tendency of the circle to indicate wholeness or completion. *Water* is a universal symbol of life and death. A desert's barrenness, devoid of water, hints at the need for water to sustain life. Its overabundance, however, in a flood or hurricane, brings destruction and death. *Fire*, a natural symbol, can indicate light and warmth, as well as sorrow or death.

Plants, animals, and humans respond to natural symbols, each in its own way. Such symbols, deeply embedded in the universal patterns that govern creation, affect human core dispositions that move us to wholeness. Natural symbols may shift focus, but their power to influence us remains.

Culturally produced symbols, like the old wooden chairs,

take their dynamism from cultural contexts, not from universal patterns. They symbolize meaningful mythical and ritualistic patterns in a family, group, or culture. The chairs were culturally produced symbols for Bertha because of what they symbolized for her.

Observation alone cannot ascertain whether something is a culturally produced symbol or a sign. I have two old black-and-white pictures in my room. The first depicts a small girl with a pretty new dress, sitting on a stool with a gold locket around her neck. Her hair is nicely combed and she is smiling. This picture, going back to the early decades of this century, has no frame. The second equally old picture has a fine frame. It depicts a young couple, hand in hand, posing for a photographer. The man is in a suit and the woman is wearing a wedding dress.

One picture is a meaningful symbol for me, the other is a sign. No one looking at the pictures could tell which is which, unless I described the story behind them. The young girl sitting on the stool is my mother. Several years ago, she gave me the picture, along with the gold locket she is wearing. I wanted to frame it. Seeing the picture with the nice frame, I bought it to frame Mom's picture. When I tried to exchange pictures, I realized I would have to cut Mom's picture to get it into the frame. I decided not to cut her picture. Liking the composition of the other picture, I left both pictures alone. Mom's picture is a powerful symbol; the other one is a sign.

Revelatory Aspects of Symbols

While signs are functional, symbols relate in some way to the ultimate. A mother kissing her child symbolizes love, just as an engagement ring symbolizes the commitment of a couple.

The symbol shows a unity with that which it symbolizes. The kiss, revealing the unity between mother and child, is not an isolated act but a vital expression of the love it symbolizes.

The ring, likewise, indicates the coming together of the engaged couple. In this way the reality expressed by the symbol and the symbol itself become one.

As distinctions between the symbol and what it symbolizes merge into one, symbolic presence becomes real presence. The kiss is more than a symbol of love; it becomes the love. The wedding ring is more than a thing made of gold, silver, or wood; it becomes a sacred expression, transcending its limits as a material thing. It discloses a real presence between two people that goes beyond space, time, and physical manifestation.

A symbol is always *revelatory*, for it opens up dimensions of the real that transcend ordinary observation. My father and mother's picture sits on my bookcase. It was taken on Thanksgiving day, five days before Dad died. It symbolically reveals the love of Dad and Mom for me and their sacrifice. People who do not know us would regard it as a sign. For me, it is a powerful symbol of our love.

The same applies to any symbol. A loving kiss unlocks and reinforces a depth of meaning that goes beyond the external act of kissing. A spousal kiss in difficult times says, "It's okay, we'll be all right." A gesture as simple as a telephone call to a hurting person provides the reassurance needed to survive a hard day. Such caring expressions hint at life's mystery. They reveal more than the external expressions convey.

Symbols point to the multifaceted mystery that they symbolize.[3] The same symbol may have different meaning for different people. After being caught in a tornado, a child in a rural neighborhood may panic whenever she sees the sky darken. A farmer living in the same area may welcome the darkening sky as a signal of oncoming rain, needed to nourish his crops. Since every symbol is embedded in the transcendent, no one meaning can capture its rich possibilities.

Every symbol touches a dimension of ultimate meaning. It links a human activity with core dispositions from which the quest for life's meaning springs.

──────────── Symbols, Context, and Meaning ────────────

Symbols allow us to search for meaning. They link with core dispositions, thus enabling us to experience core and primary mythic meaning. The oak chairs illustrate key aspects of such symbolic activity. They show how a symbol's significance is related to a mythos. For Bertha, the chairs symbolized the primary mythic meaning she found in her relationships with Tony and their family.

Initially, I did not know Bertha's story, but her words struck a deep chord within me. Originally, the chairs had secondary mythic meaning for me; afterwards, they touched a deep level of core mythic meaning. Something similar happened with the old savings book. Initially, its secondary mythic meaning related to the money the account contained. After I realized its true significance, the book symbolized primary and core mythic meaning.

Such experiences indicate how symbols relate to primary and core mythic meaning, whereas signs concern themselves with secondary mythic meaning. The oak chairs and savings book also indicate how meaning, symbols, and a symbol's context are connected.

$$meaning = symbol + context$$

Searching for *meaning* is a complex phenomenon. Initially, I regarded closing the old savings account as a functional action with a functional purpose. Its meaning involved getting the $137.38 from the account and depositing it into my trust.

My subsequent unrest revealed deeper layers of meaning. Looking at the old book while waiting for the light revealed the source of my anxiety. It (the *symbol*) had a powerful meaning because it symbolized my relationship with Dad (*context*).

The dynamic operative in this experience operates in every meaningful action. Buying the old chairs had a functional meaning for me. They would allow me to relax at my farm. For

Bertha, they had an ultimate meaning, because they symbolized her life spent with Tony and her family.

The same applies to any symbol's meaning, no matter if it is an action, an event, a thing, or a person. The pope has a different meaning for Catholics and Protestants. So does the Torah for Jews and Hindus. Two people viewing the same event may get different meanings. In each case, a symbol's meaning is directly related to its context.

A symbol is best understood when it is interpreted in its mythical context. If this context remains the same, a symbol's meaning does not vary. Hence, a wedding ring has positive meaning for a married couple if their relationship remains vibrant.[4]

A symbol's meaning and power are closely related. If its meaning changes, so does its power. After Stanley, my father, died, Mom gave me his gold ring with a ruby stone. She said,

When your father was sixteen, he had to quit school to help support his family by working in their store. Several years later, the bank president, recognizing his intelligence, wanted to train him in the banking business. Your Dad felt obliged to work in the store, so he declined this offer.

By the time Stanley was eighteen, he saved enough money to buy the ring. It was special to him. It symbolized his adulthood and his commitment to his family. After we married, I often looked at it, wondering what he might have become had he pursued his education or followed the career in banking. The ring reminds me of the kind of man he was. Now I want you to have it.

After Mom's explanation, the ring's power changed for me. Her words gave depth to its significance, as it took on a far more profound meaning.

The power of any culturally produced symbol can change, for a symbol's power is affected by the mythos and rituals within which it operates. When these perspectives shift, the symbol's significance changes. The hammer and sickle once symbolized the Soviet Union's power. As this nation broke apart from within, this symbol lost its power, because the country's mythos changed.

Changing mythical contexts in the business environment require companies to shift focus. Many large corporations, once top-heavy with bureaucracy and multileveled organizations, have downsized. Complex organizations, once symbolic of successful companies, no longer hold the same significance. Shifting market forces require companies to develop alternative work modes. Changes unknown a few years ago, intensify as technology becomes more sophisticated.

The world is becoming more unified through rapid travel, technology, immigration, and increased cooperation between nations. A better appreciation of the ways that mythos influences symbolic actions will enhance communication in a global culture and open up new possibilities for the third millennium.

10

Scholarships, Rings, and Things: Faith and the Mosaic of Meaning

Looking at the old savings book caused me to reflect on meaning and to consider faith's role in our search for meaning in the new millennium. This chapter addresses the faith question. It considers faith and mythos, different faith dimensions, intuition and faith, community and faith, and faith as completing our mosaic of meaning.

Faith and Mythos

In some way, faith always involves saying yes to a mythos. My childhood faith in my father strengthened as our relationship solidified. It was my response to the mythos that developed between us.

Faith springs from relationships that engender confidence, respect, and trust. When doubts arise in close relationships, we are inclined to deny questionable behavior, like the accusation that a trusted child has stolen money or a loving spouse has been unfaithful. Only when we are given strong verification of such claims does faith in a person change.

Like mythos, faith is operative in functional and ultimate matters. People planning to build a house usually choose a builder because of the contractor's reputation. One person may put faith in company A, while a second individual may prefer company B. Such preferences happen because peoples' mythical perspectives differ. Different perceptions also exist in the case of faith in a doctor, attorney, social worker, teacher, parent, friend, business associate, work group, or rescue team.

But faith often operates on a level deeper than the trust we have in professional workers. The community near St. Mark's Church believes that its parishioners will support them in difficult circumstances. This faith was rewarded when a tornado devastated several blocks near the church. Immediately, church members provided assistance to the afflicted.

Faith in more ultimate matters is influenced by different mythical perspectives. The Adams family shares its time, talent, and possessions with parents, grandparents, brothers, sister, nieces, and nephews whenever a member struggles with job loss, sickness, or death. The Bennie family is different. In difficult times, they need to look beyond the family for help.

Since mythical perspectives are rich and complex, faith responses vary, as in the case of Connie, who is drawn to the Third Church of God, whose mythos satisfies her needs. Her attraction rests on the way this congregation interprets Scripture.

She accepts every word of the Bible as literally coming from God. She has faith in the Church of God, because it interprets the Bible this way, but she gives little attention to a nearby congregation that stresses the deeper meaning of biblical passages, not their literal interpretation.

Different Faith Dimensions

Secondary faith is connected with skill in performing functional tasks. My father taught me how to fix things, build play boxes, and put together swing sets. He constructed a shower room in our basement, repaired support beams of our house with concrete piers, and replaced our drive run.

As a child, I believed my Dad could fix anything. If he had

failed to build the shower or repair the concrete piers, I would not have had such faith in his functional skills, even though I loved him deeply. My secondary faith rested on his skills, not his personality.

Primary faith is rooted more in people. I first encountered it through my parents. Their faith set the tone for my basic beliefs. As I grew, this faith was reinforced or challenged by my successes and disappointments. During childhood, several events shook my faith. When I was seven, Louis, my oldest uncle, returned from a war zone after being tortured by the enemy and left for dead. He never completely recovered from this ordeal.

In the ninth grade, Jimmy, my youngest uncle, was killed in a car accident on New Year's Eve. Not long afterwards, Dad required hospitalization. His partial paralysis threw our family into uncertainty. These events jolted my rudimentary faith, and doubts emerged.[1]

These traumatic experiences were offset by happy, joyous times. Picnics, hikes, and family vacations broadened my horizons, giving me an appreciation of nature, the universe, and other cultures. Working at my father's store taught me to be at ease with strangers. In college, my faith solidified as I learned to put my trust in God.

Although primary faith tends to revolve around people, it may exist also in situations that involve functional work. This happened with Mike soon after he underwent an IRS tax audit. When his accountant failed to support him, Mike went to a tax preparing agency, where Bernice did his taxes. He had faith in her because of her professional expertise, but even more because she cared.

Core faith links us with a dimension of reality that is connected with the origin of the universe and humankind. The basic beliefs of all religious traditions rely on core faith, whose source is a power beyond us. A sunset or a mountain often inspires such faith, as we recognize their beauty or grandeur, while conscious of our limitations.

Core faith enables us to go beyond what is believable on the level of primary faith. While positive human relationships involve primary faith, they also open up pathways for core faith by enabling us to profess belief that transcends our faith in fallible humans. Primary faith relationships lead us to core faith, based on a transcendent life source, which religious traditions associate with God. This life source is integral to our search for meaning.

Making sense of life means accepting insights that come from core faith. World religions teach that life is transformed at death, when the full flowering of our meaning is manifested.

Faith and Intuition

There is a close relationship between faith and intuition. Intuition, another form of knowing, is deeper than rational analysis.[2] It is evident when we know a particular action is correct, even though reason cannot explain it.[3]

A counselor sometimes relies on intuition when advising a client about a difficult situation. It moves us to see parts within a larger whole by pointing to connections that elude rational analysis. It urges us to go beyond the present situation and connect with energies flowing from core dispositions. This process allows such energies to jell into our primary and core mythos.

The intuitive way of knowing is as real as rational thought. It enabled Einstein to develop his general theory of relativity. It gives us insights about loved ones and provides clues when something is wrong. It hints at a transcendent realm that roots our actions, beliefs, and traditions. It helps crystallize our beliefs, thereby making faith possible.[4] It plays a key role in situations that require faith. I trusted my intuition when Sam, the head coach at a high school, asked me to coach the boy's freshman basketball team.

In early practices, I saw great talent on this team. Sam told me to keep fourteen players. Selecting this number should have been easy, for there were just fourteen talented freshmen. My decision was difficult, however, for one other player, named Jim, showed real promise. He was a small, thin boy, about 4' 11" tall. Jim's arms weren't strong enough to get the ball to the hoop, when he tried a one-handed jump shot. In contrast, his long arms, legs, and fingers enabled him to palm the ball and dribble circles around the other players.

I told Sam I intended to keep fifteen players. He said, "You can't, we only have fourteen uniforms." I described Jim's potential, insisting that he get another uniform. Sam replied, "I'll give you an old uniform, but it won't be the same style as the other ones." Jim stayed on the team and wore the old uniform.

By year's end, he began to grow. Before the next fall's practice began, Jim had grown to 5'10", and he started at point guard as a sophomore. In his junior year, he was 6'4" tall. He led his team to the state championship in each of his last two high school years. At graduation, Jim received a college scholarship. He starred in college, was drafted by an NBA team and played for six seasons.

If I had followed my reason and considered only his talent as a freshman, I would have cut Jim from the team. My intuition hinted at his potential, determination, and commitment to the game. This intuition was expressed as faith in Jim as a person and potential basketball star. I wonder what would have happened if I had not trusted my intuition. Would Jim have quit after the freshman year and never pursued basketball?

Intuition moves people to believe in a reality beyond rational comprehension that is associated with primary and core faith. Kierkegaard's "leap of faith" speaks of such faith, usually referred to as religious faith.[5]

Religious faith inclines people to believe in a transcendent source of meaning, generally associated with God—Yahweh, Allah, or Manitou. It moves them to believe that God created the world and keeps it in existence.

As East and West come together in the twenty-first century,

different mythical perspectives in each tradition will enable humankind to fashion a more humane society. This can happen if intuitive and rational ways of knowing blend into a fresh synthesis.

Faith and Community[6]

Faith develops in the interaction between people. In a business where trust and expertise predominate, employees usually have faith in their employers. Such faith is essential for efficient working operations. In a family, church, or friendship, faith emerges from mutual love and respect. Such faith is necessary to pursue our search for meaning.

Mythos deeply influences the faith that emerges from the give and take between people and events. Reflections on my mother's high school years indicate the multifaceted dimensions operative in faith's response to mythos. Mom loved her first three years in a coeducational high school with students from the same socioeconomic background as hers. In her senior year, this school became an all-boys institution. Mom joined other girls in her class and transferred to an all-girls school, which up to that time had been a private school.

Years later, when I was in my junior year of high school, Mom went with me to select a *class ring.* She bought me an expensive one and did the same thing for my two sisters and brother. When grandchildren came, Mom also purchased their class rings. After the youngest grandchild graduated, she explained why she wanted every family member to have a nice high school ring.

Mom began, "In my senior year, our family could not afford the price of my class ring. I was the only graduating senior without one. After a few classmates chided me for not having a ring, I resolved never to allow this to happen in my family."

The absence of this symbol on her finger affected Mom's mythos. It strengthened her faith in herself and built confidence in her children and grandchildren. Giving us a ring rewarded her faith and affirmed every family member.

Over the years, Mom occasionally spoke of the girl in her senior class who had received a college scholarship. During Dad's last sickness, I took Dad and Mom to visit their childhood homes. During our trip, the girl that got a scholarship came up in our conversation. When her name surfaced, Mom told me that she also received a scholarship. Surprised, I answered, "All these years, you never told me that you got one."

Mom continued, "In my senior year, the principal called me into her office and said, "Olivia, you have done extremely well since you came here. The faculty has awarded you a college scholarship that this school gives every year to an outstanding senior."

Overjoyed, Mom went home and told her mother. After a long pause, Grandma said, "Olivia, we are too poor for you to go to college. There is not enough money to buy the clothes and books you will need for college. Besides, we depend on you to support our family." The next day, Mom declined the college scholarship.

After Mom told me the story, she said, "It was okay. If I had taken the scholarship, I would not have met your father, and you would not be here."

Mom's mythos never expressed any regret over the ring or a college scholarship. She took them to a deeper level of primary and core faith, knowing that she had acted admirably in placing her family ahead of a ring or professional achievement. Her core faith in God enabled her to transcend personal disappointment for a higher good.

Mom's faith, honed by such experiences, shaped her subsequent attitudes and actions. It was integral to her life and brought countless blessings to our family.

—— Faith: Completing the Mosaic of Meaning ——

Secondary, primary, and core faith are intimately related, one blending into the other. The basic dynamics underlying such faith responses relate to the mythos from which they emerge.

Hence, an employer's faith in a contractor's ability rests on how the employer regards the contractor's skills. Faith in a child's veracity depends on mythical perspectives underlying parental knowledge of the child's trustworthiness. Faith in the universe, humankind, or religious revelation springs from an individual's core mythos.

All faith responses involve a blending of different faith modes. Selecting a contractor depends on more than worker's skills (secondary faith). It includes the employer's personal regard for the individual (primary faith). Both modes are interdependent. Regardless of a contractor's skills, an untrustworthy individual will not be hired. This happened in the Smythe family. When looking for a contractor to do a repair job on their porch, they discovered that a man who formerly had remodeled their kitchen later had robbed their home. He had performed well as a carpenter but poorly as a man. Needless to say, he was not interviewed for the job.

Connections exist also between primary and core faith. Faith in parents, coming from a lifetime of love and trust, sets the stage for trust in God. Such core faith is influenced also by positive experiences with friends, ministers, and churches.

In our search for meaning, we strive to fulfill urges coming from core dispositions. They move us to address fundamental questions about birth, identity, happiness, suffering, and death. Our efforts, however, never fully satisfy the human quest. Instead, they lead us to see that faith in a transcendent reality is at the center of our search for meaning. This was manifested during my father's last illness.

During Dad's fifty-nine days in the hospital, his body deteriorated greatly. His arms became fragile relics of once-powerful limbs. His skin, thin as tissue paper, was black and blue from the numerous intravenous lines. He lingered on silently, never complaining about the intense suffering he patiently endured. Long, dark nights blended into longer days, often spent in silence. As I sat by his bed, I wondered, "Why?"

After Dad had one particularly difficult day, I stayed with

him until late in the evening. Upon returning to my residence, I sat alone on the floor in my room. I cried and screamed, "Why him, God? He is such a good man." I beat my fist on the floor to the litany of "Why him?"

No answer came, but my faith pictured Jesus in the Garden of Gethsemane. He asked a similar question. I thought, "If there was meaning in Jesus' suffering there must be meaning in Dad's." I didn't know what that meaning was, but it must exist.

The silent trauma, seeing my father endure excruciating pain, was broken by the faint hope that core faith offered. It gave me confidence in a tomorrow filled with life, freedom, and hope. Without it, I don't know what I would have done.

To complete the mosaic of meaning involves moving toward core faith, which is central to our search for meaning.[7] Such faith is the capstone, enabling us to live a balanced life that finds partial fulfillment on this earth and complete happiness in eternity.

Conclusion

The new millennium offers us the opportunity to look deeper into ourselves. Examining the question of meaning and the ways that myth, ritual, and symbol structure our search for meaning, enables us to glean fresh insights into ourselves and our role in the world.

In our journey, we aim to fulfill ourselves as persons. Today's opportunities never will be repeated. Reflecting on our life meaning indicates the importance of making the most of every second, of every moment, of every day.

A better understanding of mythos and ritual helps us to approach situations with greater wisdom. In the concrete dealings of everyday life, an intuitive grasp of a person or group's mythos assists our communications and decision making. In preparing for a job interview, it is wise to ascertain the company's mythos. Often a person seeking a job can get help from the company's published literature, goals, advertising, employees, and rituals.

In giving advice to a colleague, it is well to ascertain key elements of this person's mythos. This might involve whether the individual is married, divorced, or single. It also means ascertaining specific aspects of the person's problem. The more we appreciate another's mythos, the easier it is to help the individual.

In personal matters involving parents, spouses, children, siblings, and friends, it helps to reflect on the mythical perspectives involved. Often, reflecting on people's ritual patterns helps us appreciate their mythos if it differs from ours. Such efforts lead to more effective communication and happier lives. Ascertaining a group's or individual's mythos includes assimilating facts, but is more dependent on our intuitive grasp of deeper mythical elements operative in each situation. This requires time and experience, but is worth the effort.

In times of joy and sorrow, it is wise to acknowledge our gifts, admit our limits, and open ourselves to the transcendent. In this way we live in this wonderful world, open to a transcendent source of happiness that invites us to search for the full meaning of our lives.

Important symbols, like the old savings book, remind us of who we are in our life journey. As I look again at the old book, I thank Dad for the love and wisdom it represents. It symbolizes my mythical search and the various experiences that have shaped me.

I now pause in silent gratitude and invite you to do the same. Keep your symbol close at hand and occasionally look at it. In the new millennium we need such symbols to tell us who we are and what we are called to become. They are beacons in our search for ultimate meaning and fulfillment.

Notes

Chapter 1

1. Viktor Frankl, *Man's Search for Meaning* (New York: Simon & Schuster, 1963), 176.

2. Ibid., 178–183.

3. For a discussion of the encoding process in the instinctual activities of animals, see Tom F. Driver, *The Magic of Ritual* (San Francisco: HarperSanFrancisco, 1991), 12–23.

4. Culture shapes the way we ask basic life questions. Many people living in Third World poverty need to concentrate on survival needs, like gathering food, providing shelter, and protecting themselves. The poverty and unrest in such circumstances may make quality relationships between people difficult. The desire to survive motivates their efforts, which require activities associated with secondary mythic meaning. Their motivation springs from a deeper need, rooted in primary and core mythic meaning. While hoping for a better tomorrow for family and tribe (primary mythic meaning), they often find hope in cultural and religious beliefs (core mythic meaning).

5. See Robert J. Hater, "Philosophical Implications of Gordon W. Allport's Theory of the Person" (Ph.D. dissertation, St. John's University, New York, 1967).

Chapter 2

1. Philosophers, holy men and women, theologians, and people of various ages and backgrounds have reflected on life's meaning. Their unique circumstances, perspectives, and outlooks influenced their conclusions, and the paradigms they developed. The staying power of a paradigm depends on its congruence with objective evidence, personal experience, and historical data that transcend centuries and cultures. See Thomas Kuhn, *Structure of Scientific Revolutions* (Chicago: University of Chicago, 1965).

2. Freedom is closely associated with a person's ability to actualize one's human potential. It includes the relational possibility of fulfilling deep dimensions of one's personhood. A close relationship exists between freedom and creativity. Both presume the boundaries of age, race, culture, talent, and social

possibilities that the individual enjoys. See Nicolas Berdyaev, *The Beginning and the End* (New York: Harper & Brothers, 1952).

3. See Gabriel Marcel, *Being and Having, An Existentialist Diary* (New York: Harper & Row, 1965), 100.

4. In *Being and Having* (p. 141), Marcel distinguishes problem from mystery.

5. Immanuel Kant describes space and time as categories of human reason in the *Critique of Pure Reason*. Fixed, "a priori forms" categorize data received through the senses. Kant's conclusions let us view these forms as file folders, into which appropriate data are divided. These forms exist before any sense data enter them. See Immanuel Kant, *The Critique of Pure Reason* (London: J. M. Dent & Sons, 1959).

6. Ibid.

7. Viktor Frankl. *Man's Search for Meaning* (1939; New York: Simon & Schuster, 1963), 188. In this expression, "logos" implies a deeper context of meaning that transcends logical categories or rational analysis. It is used differently than the term "logos" in chapter 5 n. 2.

8. This section on Native American beliefs and rituals is not intended to over-glamorize their lives. Many of their fundamental beliefs have been lost, largely the result of centuries of colonization. Serious efforts are being made today by Native American leaders to reintroduce many of their people to their fundamental beliefs. This is meeting with various degrees of success, as Native Americans strive to reestablish an identity and a pride that have been seriously diminished over past centuries. Native Americans, like the rest of us in the Americas, are inundated with secular values. Mutual cooperation is the best way for maximizing the benefits inherent in their traditions and in Western society.

9. Logical positivists presume a materialistic perspective. They advocate a worldview based primarily on logic and language. In their view, language has meaning if it can be verified empirically. Hence, if the statement "God exists" cannot be verified by logical categories or sense data, it is meaningless. Therefore, statements of metaphysics, religion, and ethics generally are meaningless, because they employ nonverifiable language. Logical positivism holds that the structure of language gives a picture of the world's structure. For them, the world's meaning structure excludes experiences that go beyond those capable of empirical verification. Logical positivists leave little room for primary or core mythic meaning. Their realm of discourse is secondary mythic meaning. This philosophical approach, which originated in Europe, was strong in many U.S. universities after World War II. See Alfred Jules Ayer, *Language, Truth and Logic* (New York: Dover Publications, 1946); idem, *Logical Positivism* (New York: Free Press, 1959).

10. See Roger Schmidt, *Exploring Religion,* 2nd ed. (Belmont, Calif.: Wadsworth, 1988), 7–11. In analyzing issues surrounding religion, Schmidt states, "For our purposes, religion is defined as a human seeking and responding to what is experienced as holy" (p. 11). The notion of "holy" is associated with what is described in this book under the umbrella of the "ultimate."

11. See Gordon W. Allport, *The Individual and His Religion* (New York: Macmillan, 1974), chapter 3, "The Religion of Maturity" (pp. 59ff.); idem, *Personality: A Psychological Interpretation* (New York: Henry Holt, 1937), chapter 8.

12. Allport describes these three dimensions as ego extension, self-objectification, and a unifying philosophy of life (see *Individual and His Religion*, 60).

13. Allport describes this form of Ego-Extension in terms of the need to develop a "variety of psychogenic interests . . . which concern themselves with ideal objects and values beyond the range of viscerogenic desire" (*Individual and His Religion*, 60).

14. Ibid., 61ff.

15. Ibid.

16. Ibid, 64.

17. See P. Teilhard de Chardin, *The Phenomenon of Man* (New York: Harper & Row, 1961); idem, *Building the Earth* (New York: Discus Books, Avion Books, 1969); idem, *The Divine Milieu* (New York: Harper & Row, 1960).

Chapter 3

1. Language makes it hard to describe the spiritual dimension of the person without falling into some kind of dualism. The expression "enfleshed" indicates that the core of the person is spiritual, so as to avoid the trap of seeing the spirit as dwelling in the body as in a container. While on earth, the spirit-body is one, although the spiritual dimension transcends the confines of the body and is able to communicate on a spiritual level with realities beyond the body.

2. In normal circumstances a healthy body enhances the spirit. Diet, exercise, and sleep play important roles in maintaining a vibrant spirit. During sickness or when death approaches, bodily functions are limited. Often, these times reveal clearly that the spirit depends on the body but transcends it. I saw this during my father's last year.

3. Viktor Frankl, *Man's Search for Meaning* (New York: Simon & Schuster, 1963), 60–61.

4. Greek stoics spoke of *logoi spermatikoi,* or seminal words. These influence our dealings with the world. Plato believed that we preexist in a "world of ideas," the realm of the "truly real." Here the true, the good, and the beautiful exist. Such ideas or forms are reflected, only faintly, in this earthly world. At birth, we forget most of this preexistent realm and enter a shadow world. Through education, we remember some of what we forgot from the world of ideas.

Jesus and Philo the Jew believed that humans are made in God's image. Within each individual, God's spirit dwells, giving motivation and direction. Carl Jung spoke of archetypes or archetypal patterns as universal dispositions of the mind. For him, they are instinctual orientations, just as natural to humans as is the instinct moving birds to construct nests. See Carl Jung, "Approaching the Unconscious," in *Man and His Symbols* (New York: Dell, 1968), 58.

5. The expression "core dispositions" is an intellectual construct used to indicate those inner tendencies arising from deep within each person that set basic directions for life. They are not to be understood in a physical sense, like an arm or leg.

6. The person is an organic unity. Some life dynamics come from core dispositions; others from organic dispositions because humans are animals; still others because a reciprocity exists between the person and the world in the process of human actualization.

Core dispositions are unique prerogatives of people as human beings. They include the search for meaning, beauty, and truth.

Organic dispositions belong to humans because they are animals. They include desires for survival, sexuality, and nourishment. To be fully actualized in the human person, they need to be realized within the context of human morality and responsibility. Hence, the sexual desire is actualized maturely and responsibly within the deeper context of spousal love.

Actualized dispositions flow from reciprocity of the person and life experiences. They motivate humans to action because of previous interactions between core/organic dispositions and the external world. Hence, a healthy family environment, where a child is nurtured and loved, disposes the individual to reach out to life in a positive and confident way.

Core dispositions are essential in the human pursuit of meaning. These are filtered through inherited *organic (animal) dispositions,* such as those that move all animals to survive, to eat, and to engage in sexual activity. Core human dispositions give order and clarity to such urges coming from our animal nature. To fulfill ourselves as person, however, requires *actualization of core dispositions* in reciprocity with the external world.

7. Core dispositions belong to humans as enfleshed spirits. To further clarify them, we consider their relationship to "conscience," which is a spiritual voice within us pointing to the difference between right and wrong. It inclines us to make good moral decisions.

Conscience is rooted in core dispositions, which incline us toward what is good for ourselves as persons. Conscience specifies this "good" in relation to this or that particular moral action. Like conscience, which provides moral urgings, core dispositions provide broader urgings that help people fulfill themselves as persons.

8. This is particularly true of the Christian tradition.

9. Jung, *Man and His Symbols* (New York: Dell, 1968), 259.

10. In commenting on Jung's view, Leonard J. Biallas says: "Jung referred to those images that regulate the forces of the psyche as 'archetypes.' The archetypes are analogous to the instincts, but operate in the psyche instead of the body. They are inherited primordial images that emerge from the unconscious to bring the human psyche some insight and awareness into the constantly repeated experiences of humanity . . ." (*Myths, gods, heroes, and saviors* [Mystic, Conn.: Twenty-Third Publications, 1986], 31).

11. Jung proposes that "acquired characteristics" were incorporated into a species' gene pool. Our approach explains the similar patterns through the world, not by "primordial" memories contained within the collective unconscious of the race but by similar dynamic core dispositions, which are focused by various cultures. Such cultures interpret the dynamism of the core dispositions in light of particular circumstances and times.

Jung related archetypal patterns to the collective unconscious, which contains some ancestral experiences, or "archaic remnants" inherited into the gene structure of subsequent generations. See Jung, *Man and His Symbols.* It is equally possible that the collective unconscious operates in accordance with core dispositions, as these focus differently within a group, family, society, or nation. It can be questioned whether archaic remains, existing in the human psyche as a result of humankind's past history, are needed to explain similar patterns in myths, religion, dreams, fantasies, and literature. Each group's collective imagination, moved by dynamism from core dispositions, arranges into similar patterns the data received from the group's cultural experiences. The similarities result from common patterns governing this process.

12. See Mircea Eliade, *Myths, Dreams and Mysteries* (New York: Harper & Row, 1969).

13. Aristotle and Thomas Aquinas said that our quest for happiness is the most basic human desire. According to them, everything we do in life we see under some aspect of the "good," which enhances our happiness. For example, even though an employee knows it is wrong to steal from an employer, the person may do so nonetheless, seeing the money taken under some aspect of a particular good, like buying an automobile, going on a vacation, or paying off a debt.

14. *Rig Veda* X, *cxxix* contains a Hindu creation myth. It expresses similar elements as in the first Genesis creation account, where God's spirit moved over the waters. The Hindu myth teaches that neither being nor non-being is the source of the world, for each requires the other. Both accounts hit at the common source of meaning. This myth attributes the earth's origins to a force that transcends being and non-being. The myth hints at the presence of a transcendent source of all becoming—a fountainhead of meaning and a source of unity. From this source meaning and fulfillment originate. No words exist for this source. See Barbara C. Sproul, *Primal Myths* (San Francisco: HarperSanFrancisco, 1993), 183–84.

15. Genesis 3:15 hints at the messianic hope, which includes a woman's vital role.

16. See Brother David, O.S.B., "The Biblical View of the Cosmos," in *Cosmic Piety*, ed. Christopher Derrick (New York: P. J. Kennedy & Sons, 1965), 21–23.

17. Sproul, *Primal Myths*, 179–80.

18. Similar patterns are found in dreams, fairy tales, ritual activities, novels, art, poetry, and personal activities. They indicate many ways that we strive for happiness.

19. See Augustine, *Confessions of St. Augustine*, trans. Albert C. Outler, in *Library of Christian Classics*, vol. 7, *Augustine, Confessions and Enchridion* (Philadelphia: Westminster, 1955), book 1, chapter 1, p. 31.

Chapter 4

1. Instinct serves this function in other animals.

2. See Robert J. Hater, *New Visions, New Directions* (Allen, Tex.: Thomas More Press, 1994), 2–3.

3. Ibid., 2ff.

4. If a child provides money to care for an elderly parent primarily to fulfill a duty, the motivation is not as deep as if his/her actions are performed out of abiding love.

5. Community includes two or more persons relating to one other on a regular, responsible, and ultimate level over a period of time.

6. This section is an adaption of a section in my *New Vision, New Directions* (pp. 43–49).

7. See pp. 5–11 above. This section discusses the three modes of mythic meaning. These modes are intellectual constructs, not existing as such in the

human person. They are a shorthand way to categorize certain dispositions in human becoming and illustrate the complex relationship between an individual and the wider world.

Chapter 5

1. *Mythoi*, the plural of mythos, refers to the mythos of several groups or individuals. *Mythical elements* are particular aspects of a mythos. *Mythical perspective* means viewing a situation through the lens of mythos. It is not the same as a logical perspective, which considers a situation from a rational or objective vantage point, whereas the former views it from a holistic perspective. The mythical vantage point often includes all three modes of mythic meaning.

2. *Mythos* embraces what is of value and meaning in a society's experiences, as these values and meaning contexts emerge over time. Mythos often is expressed in poetry, art, metaphor, drama, song, ritual, stories, and other modes of human communication. See Bernard E. Meland, *Faith and Culture* (Carbondale, Ill.: Southern Illinois University Press, 1972).

Logos is the realm of rational discourse and analytic thought. It functions within the context of rationality. The conceptual perspectives that *logos* employs enable us to plan, reflect, build models, and judge. Construction of models is possible because of the realm of *logos*, which operates on the conscious level.

3. *Mythos* relates to a deeper mode of human response, usually operating below the conscious level. Its realm embraces the whole person, including reason. Any *mythos* can be rationally analyzed, but not developed by rational planning alone. Every *mythos* emerges out of the give and take of people over time. See Bernard E. Meland, *Fallible Forms and Symbols* (Philadelphia: Fortress Press, 1976), 102–3.

Ethos refers to a particular orientation embodied in a society's or group's *mythos*. *Ethos* dictates approved and unapproved norms of conduct. These norms flow from a group's *mythos*, which underlies a group's moral standards. *Ethics* is a systematic analysis and interpretation of the moral perspectives, principles, and practices that emerge from a group's *mythos* and *ethos*. Ethics uses logical thought processes to clarify approved norms of behavior, social conduct, and personal morality.

4. A distinction can be made between implicit and explicit mythos. An *implicit mythos* is not clearly articulated by the group or individual involved. In other words, it is an assumed attitude, setting the tone for the people involved. Serving as a motivator for action, its orientation remains largely on a preconscious level. A *mythos* becomes *explicit* when certain key elements of the mythos or the myth itself have been articulated consciously by those involved.

United States citizens live and act according to their cultural mythos, which implies freedom of the press and speech, obeying traffic regulations, and respecting other peoples' rights. They presume such *implicit* mythical elements, which form the underpinning of their mode of conduct, even though such elements usually are not articulated in a *explicit* way. If, however, they travel to another country where these mythical elements are absent, they become much more conscious of them. Then, their *implicit* mythos can more easily become *explicit*. *Implicit* elements of a mythos also become *explicit* through rational reflection on stories or myths. Such a process often reveals key aspects of the mythos itself.

5. Sam Keen, "Man and Myth": A Conversation with Joseph Campbell, *Psychology Today* (July 1971): 35–39, 86–95.

6. Metaphysics studies being itself. It asks questions about the nature of the "Being" that underpins all individual "beings." It concerns itself with ultimate relationships and reflects on ultimate qualities, such as goodness, truth, and beauty. All beings reflect these qualities in different ways. Metaphysics is particularly concerned with core mythic meaning. It is the proper realm in which to discuss the existence, nature, and qualities of a transcendent being, called by various names—God, Yahweh, Allah, or Manitou.

7. Richard L. Sartore, ed. *Joseph Campbell on Myth and Mythology* (Lanham, Md.: University Press of America, 1994), 4.

8. Cosmology studies the cosmos or universe. It looks at universal patterns and relationships operative in the world rather than restricting itself to a functional approach that centers on measurement and scientific data.

9. Sociology studies the origin, development, and dynamics of societies. It is concerned with human patterns of interaction and considers the organization and functions of various social groups. The sociological function of mythos establishes the underpinnings in a given society that help people in that group to satisfy basic needs coming from their core dispositions.

10. Some early societies, which embraced beautiful attitudes, teachings, and rituals, also contained distorted mythical perspectives advocating slavery, banishment, and abuse of women.

11. Psychology studies the person. Plato and Aristotle regarded humans as rational animals, and Platonic and Aristotelian psychology believed that "the psyche or soul" rooted the human being's unique gifts. Today many psychologists limit their analyses of the person to analytic, functional studies of the mind and human behavior. Much United States psychology is based on an empirical research model. Such psychology is applied science, which relies on measurement to explain human response. Psychologists more often ask why a person acts in a particular way than what it means to be a person. The psychological function of mythos helps a person fulfill one's potential as a person, by providing directions for the individual along life's path from childhood to old age.

12. Even though such a situation is dysfunctional, the mythos remains real for those involved.

Chapter 6

1. Stories differ from examples, which concern themselves with the objective.

2. *Joseph Campbell on Myth and Mythology*, ed. Richard L. Sartore (Lanham, Md.: University Press of America, 1994), 4. Campbell continues: "there are two totally different orders of mythology. There is the mythology that relates you to your nature and to the natural world, of which you're a part. And there is the mythology that is strictly sociological, linking you to a particular society" (p. 4).

3. The four functions of mythos, described in chapter 5, are also the functions of myth.

4. See *Myth, Symbol, and Reality,* ed. Alan M. Olson (Notre Dame, Ind.: University of Notre Dame Press, 1980).

5. Any deep story or myth touches the ultimate level and offers insights into life's mysteries.

6. The human search for meaning is fulfilled on an ultimate level. A group's myth offers explicit and implicit signals telling people the best ways to live.

7. Many adults, particularly of college age, begin to reexamine their life values and question the secular myth of money when given the freedom to do so in a small group setting. For them, opportunities to discuss such issues with peers are few. Many never talk about such matters with their parents.

Chapter 7

1. See Carl G. Jung, ed., *Man and His Symbols* (Garden City, N.Y.: Doubleday, 1964), 55, 67, 107.

2. The initiative for such growth began at the Second Vatican Council, or Vatican II (1960–1964). This was a worldwide meeting of bishops and the pope to set new directions for the Roman Catholic Church.

3. Church law gives the final say in parish matters to pastors. For practical purposes, however, they generally accept recommendations of lay parish commissions, organizations, and administrators, for they cannot function without them.

4. In most mythic changes, these need not develop sequentially, for human becoming does not follow logical progressions. Although all these aspects may not be evident during change, in one form or another, each is present. For an interesting analysis of dimensions similar to the ones presented here, see Stephen Larsen, *The Shaman's Doorway* (New York: Harper & Row, 1976), 35.

5. My developing forest area hinted at this quest, as new plants and animals staked out their identity. Like them, people never stop probing their identity in a changing world.

6. Orthodoxy has to do with which beliefs are considered correct or in line with the mythos of the community or group. Orthopraxis refers to correct or right practice or modes of action, consistent with the generally recognized correct teachings of the group or individual concerned.

7. As people grow older and circumstances change, their beliefs and practices often remain the same. This happens, analogously, as a forest matures. Plant and animal ecology shifts, but the overall development remains unchanged. Forces within nature dictate the right things to do in such situations.

8. It stretches the imagination to apply the objectification process to a forest area, but undeveloped land grows into a fully mature hardwood forest and plant and animal life passes through regular cycles. As each species reaches its limits, nature's process dictates new beginnings, explorations, dialogue, and maturity.

Chapter 8

1. Thomas F. Driver in *The Magic of Ritual* (San Francisco: HarperSanFrancisco, 1991), deals with the connections between human and animal rituals. He says, "Hence, we have not recognized that animals also ritualize their lives. . . . We have not understood that ritualizing is the bridge or pathway connecting animal ways to human. . . . Ritualizing is our first language, not our "mother" but our "grandmother" tongue, and as such is something we do not outgrow. . . . Ethnologists . . . have learned that animals of many different species engage in

ritual behaviors so highly patterned and so necessary for the animals' communication with each other that the scientists view them as akin to the rituals that humans perform" (pp. 13–14).

2. Some anthropologists, psychologists, philosophers, and theologians state that ritual activity emerges from the broader context of nature's propensity to ritual activity.

3. The term "ritual" is used in different ways, and no single description can convey its full meaning. Hans J. Mol relates rituals to ultimate dimensions of life by saying, "We use the term 'ritual' in the more restricted sense of the repetitive enactment of human systems of meaning" (*Identity and the Sacred* [New York: Macmillan, Free Press, 1976], 233).

4. The four functions of ritual are closely associated with the four functions of mythos, developed in chapter 5: the metaphysical, cosmological, sociological, and psychological functions. These are also functions of rituals. The specific ritual functions described in this chapter apply equally to any of them. For instance, rituals, celebrating a creation myth (metaphysical) help to root, order, change, or transcend particular aspects of personal or communal life.

A summary of the functions of ritual is contained in the following statement by Hans Mol: "Rites represent sameness in action and thereby consolidate the sameness of a system of meaning. They restore, reinforce, or redirect identity. They restore, through recommitting to memory, a system of meaning, through reabsorbing individuals into the common fabric, and through confession of sins of omission and commission. They reinforce through superimposing the constraint of social expectations, through linking the past to the present, through filling the emotional voids of instrumental and rational existence. They redirect through surrounding stressful situations with emotional support, through desacralizing an old identity, and through sacralizing a new one" (*Identity and the Sacred*, 244–45).

5. Ibid., 233.

6. Rites of rebellion occur if a person ritualizes one's rejection of a group's values. This is evident in certain music, dress, hairstyles, and shoes. It is also ritualized in flag burnings and organized rebellions against social customs.

7. Developing significant rites of passage is a great challenge in the third millennium.

8. Transcendence has a deep connection with play. Humans are naturally playful. Associated with the ultimate, play enhances a ritual's liberating function. True play always is structured. Childrens' communal play activities may seem random and disjointed, but such ritual play is actually bound tightly together. If one child violates an implicit play rule, the other children react negatively. Playfulness, even in adults, refocuses human energy in a transcendent depth.

Chapter 9

1. Research with chimpanzees and apes indicates that other animals besides humans use symbols. Symbolic activity in them, however, differs from the way humans use symbols.

2. Historically, these are represented in the "nostalgia-for-paradise" myths.

Christians believe that complete happiness will be experienced in heaven, while Buddhists look to Nirvana.

3. Every symbol symbolizes a one-to-many relationship with the reality it symbolizes. This one-to-many relationship indicates that no single dimension can exhaust the transcendent power of the symbol to reveal new facets of life.

4. Repetition of symbolic actions, like a kiss or a handshake, does not necessarily diminish their meaning. On the contrary, such actions enhance rather than weaken a symbol's meaning, as long as the mythos from which it springs remains vibrant.

Chapter 10

1. It helps to clarify the relationship between faith, doubt, and disbelief. Doubt occurs when situations arise that cause us to question a mythos. In a functional sense, this may happen when we question the veracity of advertising or wonder whether a product produces its promised results. It also occurs in ultimate matters, if we wonder about the claims of a particular religion, the existence of God, or the credibility of a church leader. Doubting usually arises when a conflict of evidence occurs between a belief and certain facts or evidence. It may occur, when a wife wonders why her husband is staying away from the home more in the evening, especially if she hears that he is having an affair with someone else. She may begin to doubt him. A believer also may doubt God's existence after experiencing a traumatic event, such as the death of a young child.

According to Gordon Allport, doubt is "an unstable or hesitant reaction, produced by the collision of evidence with prior belief, or of one belief with another" (*The Individual and His Religion* [New York: Macmillan, 1974], 100). For thinking people, doubt is normal. In some instances, rather than an obstacle to faith, it is the occasion for faith to grow and deepen.

Doubt differs from disbelief. The latter is a "negative, rejecting response or attitude" (ibid., 100). There is more finality in disbelief than in doubt. If Joe hears that his son, Mark, is embezzling company money, his first reaction might be refusal to believe the claims are true. After the rumors grow, Joe may begin to doubt Mark's truthfulness. When his son denies he is guilty, Joe may continue to believe Mark, for his doubts do not mean, necessarily that he has lost faith in Mark. Eventually, if the claims are proved to be false, Joe's faith in his son is rewarded. If, however, the claims are true, the realization may lead to a more permanent reaction in Joe, especially if such actions have occurred before. Then Joe may conclude that he cannot believe Mark any more. This thinking enters the area of disbelief.

Something similar may happen if a person doubts God. If tragedy robs a young family of a mother through a long, painful sickness, or a father through sudden death in an auto accident, some loved ones may question God. Such doubts do not automatically lead someone to reject God, but they challenge prior beliefs and provide occasions to grow in faith. A person may move beyond doubt, however, to a more definitive, rejecting attitude. This may result in the denial of God's existence or God's care for humankind. If this happens, the person is in a state of disbelief. Doubt and disbelief may happen whenever a mythos is challenged, irrespective of whether it is ultimate or functional. The result may be the deepening, realigning, refocusing, or changing of the mythos.

2. Intuition is less concrete and analytical than intellectual thought.

3. Factual knowledge alone cannot move us to say, "I believe," because faith's origin is deeper than intellectual thought. Søren Kierkegaard described it as a leap into the unknown.

4. Intuitive thought is better developed in some cultures than in others. It is especially evident in peoples that are closely tied to earth, nature, and cosmic patterns. Such connections lead to patterns that include rhythms of day and night, yearly seasons, animal cycles (hibernation, fertility, and migration), and cosmic order (planetary and galactic movements). These are central to the cultural myths of some peoples and offer insights into the human search for meaning.

Many Eastern philosophers, mystics, Native Americans, African tribes, and South Sea islanders place great credence in intuition. Western civilizations, influenced by rational, functional thought, are less inclined to accept its power.

5. See Søren Kierkegaard, *Fear and Trembling,* trans. Walter Lowrie (Garden City, N.Y.: Doubleday, Anchor Books, 1954).

6. Personal attitudes, honed in family life, are nourished by friends, school associates, neighbors, and church members. Relationships, however, involve more than ultimate experiences. They require activities associated with secondary mythic meaning, like work, which are meaningful if related to primary meaning. Core meaning underlies both primary and secondary mythic meaning. A personal relationship or work is inadequate if core meaning is absent. In addition, functional work, like typing a letter or operating a large crane, assumes ultimate proportions if done to support a family, to help alleviate humankind's suffering, or to fulfill a believer's calling to praise God through human work. Then such activities touch the core level of meaning.

OF RELATED INTEREST

crossroad